Out of My Mind

Also by Shalom Camenietzki

The Atheist's Bible: Stories
Nine Ninety-Nine: A Novel

Out of My Mind

A Psychologists's Descent into Madness and Back

Shalom Camenietzki

Printed and bound in Canada at Friesens. The text of this book is printed on 100% post-consumer recycled paper with earth-friendly vegetable-based inks.

Cover art: "Shared Madness; Locura compartida," by Alfredo Castaneda, (1938–2010). Private Collection. Photo © Christie's Images/Bridgeman Images.
Cover design: Duncan Campbell, University of Regina Press
Text design: John van der Woude, JVDW Designs
Copy editor: Kirsten Craven
Proofreader: Kristine Douaud

Library and Archives Canada Cataloguing in Publication

Title: Out of my mind : a psychologists's descent into madness and back / Shalom Camenietzki.
Names: Camenietzki, Shalom, 1939- author.
Series: Regina collection.
Description: Series statement: Regina collection
Identifiers: Canadiana (print) 20190187719 | Canadiana (ebook) 20190187743 | ISBN 9780889776890 (hardcover) | ISBN 9780889776906 (PDF) | ISBN 9780889776920 (HTML)
Subjects: LCSH: Camenietzki, Shalom, 1939-—Mental health. | LCSH: Psychologists—Canada—Biography. | LCSH: Manic-depressive persons—Canada—Biography. | LCGFT: Autobiographies.
Classification: LCC BF109.C36 A3 2020 | DDC 150.92—dc23

10 9 8 7 6 5 4 3 2 1

U OF R PRESS

University of Regina Press, University of Regina
Regina, Saskatchewan, Canada, S4S 0A2
tel: (306) 585-4758 fax: (306) 585-4699
web: www.uofrpress.ca

We acknowledge the support of the Canada Council for the Arts for our publishing program. We acknowledge the financial support of the Government of Canada. / Nous reconnaissons l'appui financier du gouvernement du Canada. This publication was made possible with support from Creative Saskatchewan's Book Publishing Production Grant Program.

Canada Council for the Arts Conseil des Arts du Canada Canada creative SASKATCHEWAN

To

Georges Tamarin
Eugene Mandryk
Gary Hasey
Elliot Markson
Natasha Graham
Sagar Parikh

Doctors who eased my suffering
though I whined and wailed
that only a bullet to the head
or jumping in front of a speeding subway train
would rid me of my godawful mood swings.

Disclaimer

The names and identifying details of some of the individuals in this book have been changed to protect their privacy.

Contents

My hand is deep into my conscience,
And I speak nothing but pure truths.
—*Luís Vaz de Camões*

Chapter 1

First Descent into Hell

MY FIRST ATTACK OF BIPOLAR DISORDER, STILL called "manic-depressive illness" in 1971, took place on my first night back in Israel, a country I loved deeply. Overexcited, I lay in bed, trying in vain to fall asleep. I tossed and turned, fearful I might wake Kerstin, my wife, in bed next to me. I was thirty-two at the time, and that was my first bout of insomnia. Curious, fascinated, but unaware of the pathological nature of what was unfolding, I carried on like an astronomer scrutinizing a planet he had just discovered.

That night I was staying at my parents' home in Ramat Gan, a lovely, leafy city with well-tended parks and gardens right outside Tel Aviv. Cars travelling the street outside flashed brief swaths of light into the bedroom but were eerily quiet, as though their drivers had vowed not to disturb those blissfully asleep. As the hours passed, the dark and silent bedroom where I was supposed to be asleep made me increasingly aware of my palpitating heart.

Nothing in that day's events suggested that serious mental illness would assail me at night. In that already hot June morning, my proud parents and relatives had come to the Ben Gurion Airport to greet the pipe-smoking young psychologist with black professorial eyeglasses and matching, expertly trimmed, black beard. I had just completed two years of post-doctoral experience and was arriving with my family after six glorious weeks in Sweden, at the home of my in-laws. My wife and I well deserved that long vacation after my six years of hard work, first at the University of Kansas, and then at Topeka State Hospital, a nearby teaching facility. The meeting at the airport was the first time my parents met my wife and our two sons.

What a marvellous day! Relatives passed by my parents' apartment to meet my family and me, and I delighted in the atmosphere of joy and self-fulfilment. How many bear hugs and kisses came my way that afternoon and evening!

My relatives were eager to meet Kerstin, my fair-skinned, blond, and blue-eyed Swedish wife, who, despite the Reform conversion she had initiated, was, in their eyes, an authentic *shikseh*, with few chances of ever becoming equal to Jews by birth. Bustling with fresh fruit, cups of coffee, and homemade cakes, my exulting mother tried hard to convey to Kerstin that she and our extended family welcomed the newcomer.

Even though my mother didn't mention how proud she was of her sons, doctors both of them, she brought up terms like "doctor's appointments," and, an hour later, "private practice." She regarded her sons' accomplishments as tribute to the ways they had been brought up, especially since both my parents had only grade-school education. Yet my parents easily grasped how my brother, a cardiologist, could support a family of five by treating heart conditions. As for obscure ailments like psychological disorders, my parents had never understood why it had taken me nine years to study commonplaces like lousy moods or excessive worrying. In fact, only decades later, when I began renovating my Toronto home from top to bottom but paying contractors out of pocket, did my father heave a sigh of relief, as he had dreaded that psychiatric illness would one day incapacitate me completely.

Meyer, my brother, practised cardiology in Rio de Janeiro, where he too had married a *shikseh*, Helia, whose father and grandfather had been ardent communists, just like my brother, who in the forties and fifties called himself "a professional revolutionary" as he painstakingly fomented a Bolshevik-like revolution in Brazil.

Having despaired of falling asleep that night, I rolled out of bed, then strode into my mother's kitchen. I sat in the dark and chain-smoked. "Why was I sleepless," I asked myself, and just one word explained it all: *excitement*. I was excited to be back in Israel with my young family. I had an exciting job awaiting me at the Shalvatah Psychiatric Hospital, an institution affiliated with Tel Aviv University. Once the dust of readjusting to life in Israel had settled, I told myself, I would start writing short stories. As Kerstin knew, living in Israel and writing in Hebrew loomed high in my daydreams of becoming a successful writer and a practising clinical psychologist. Even before we got married, I had made life in Israel a precondition of my marriage. To soothe my misgivings, I had convinced myself that, with my support and my friends' help, she would one day come to terms with life in a country frequently at war, where our sons would at the end of high school be drafted into the army.

Chain-smoking, I began planning what to do the next day, and decided to take my family on a tour of Tel Aviv and Jaffa. I had resigned myself to the idea of not sleeping a wink that night when I heard my mother at the entrance to her kitchen calling me "Shoolemshee"—my childhood nickname. Decades later, in 2006, a semi-autobiographical novella of mine, *The Star of Childhood Memories*, was published. In it I depicted the narrator's mother as a lukewarm, barely demonstrative, and hard-to-reach woman. She now surprised me by sounding so genuinely concerned about my sleepless night.

"Yes, Imma," I replied. Having been born in Brazil and early on raised mostly by a black Brazilian maid, my first language is Portuguese, not my parents' Yiddish. But in the last twenty years my parents and I had been speaking Hebrew most of the time, as my parents were passionate Zionists, who insisted on speaking nothing but that language. We invoked Portuguese or Yiddish expressions only when hilarious phrases occurred to us.

My mother turned on the ceiling light, and a frigid, milky, fluorescent light at once lit up the kitchen's walls, making me blink. "It looks like you can't fall asleep," she said after sitting down on a chair facing mine. Her wizened cheeks looked flabby and porous, and her lips had almost disappeared. She wasn't wearing her dentures, and her toothless gums showed.

"I was thinking," I answered. For reasons I wasn't aware of then, I hardly ever opened up to my mother.

"You must be excited," my mother said. "Your children look marvellous! And so many changes in your life! Only twenty-four hours ago you were in Sweden, but now you're where you belong." My mother, in her twenties, had been a *khalutzah*, a woman pioneer. She had left Poland in the early twenties to build a secular Jewish homeland in Palestine. After years of back-breaking work, my parents moved to Brazil, where they lived for twenty-five years. At the time of our conversation, she had been living in Israel close to twenty years.

"Yes, I am excited," I concurred. "Tomorrow I'll be taking Kerstin and the boys on a tour. A few days later, I'll be calling the hospital."

"Take your time, son," she said, her voice a trifle challenging. "The hospital won't run away. Instead, help your wife fall in love with our beautiful country." She reached for my cigarettes and lit one. "I'm not sure I like your beard," she chuckled. "It makes you look like a rabbi. As you know, I've never been keen on religion!"

"Why don't you go back to bed, Imma? You had a long, tiring day. It's soon breakfast time, and there will be six of us at the table."

She lifted her eyebrows, then let them settle down. "For six years I've been waiting to have you back where you belong. And your baby son is so cute! Like his mother, he's fair-skinned, blond, and blue-eyed." She paused, probably marvelling at her falling in love with a Nordic-looking grandson at first sight.

She sighed as she said, "Sleep can wait awhile. At any rate, I have sleeping pills my doctor prescribed. Why don't you try one? In twenty minutes you'll be sound asleep."

I thought it over, as on only two occasions had I taken tranquilizers. The first was on the night before the defence of my doctoral dissertation. A close friend had urged me to take a Valium, since I had two babies who quite often woke me up at night. "You'll be too tired to face a committee of five professors," my friend commented.

And now my mother was urging me to take a pill in order to cope with insomnia. How prophetic! Over the next four decades, I would, at times, gulp down up to fifteen pills a day. Ambivalent and hesitant, I took my mother's pill and soon fell asleep.

My first white night was not the only faint indication of the serious illness I would contend with for decades. Soon after graduating from the University of Kansas, I became distressingly anxious, but despite much soul-searching I remained woefully unaware of the triggers that had precipitated my suffering. I called Erik Wright, the head of the clinical psychology program at the University of Kansas that I had attended and asked to see him "for personal reasons." I had always felt at ease with Erik, as I had studied hard throughout graduate school, since I ached to graduate as soon as possible and launch my psychologist-cum-writer career.

Erik invited me to his home. I described my sudden, inexplicable anxiety, and he asked a few sympathetic questions. I wondered aloud whether I had become anxious over my plans to return to Israel. He offered no suggestions or recommendations but handed me a single tranquilizer, to help me calm down, as he put it. I felt thankful for his attentive listening and his refraining from explaining my distress away. In fact, that meeting reassured me so much that for over a year I experienced no upsets or psychic pain.

Another revealing event took place while I was vacationing in Sweden, a year after meeting with Erik Wright. My memory of those events is dim. What my wife told me was that one night I woke up and, in a frenzy, shattered a couple of window panes in an attempt to exit the bedroom we were sleeping in. The morning after is what I recall vividly, as my mother-in-law accompanied me as I lugged the broken window to a handyman's workshop. At the time, I thought I must have been in the throes of a distressing nightmare. Though my in-laws never uttered a word about the incident, they did worry about my health, as Kerstin told me years later, since I was about to inaugurate a new life in Israel.

Only retrospectively, with the distance of many years, did I realize that the above-mentioned events were subtle precursors to my frightful illness. Bipolar disorder is, after all, a serious mental illness, and no wonder I, and later on my doctors, didn't consider that diagnosis and its malignant implications. I had, moreover, been a successful student and a promising young psychologist, so that the last thing to dawn on me was that madness was slowly, but inexorably, making ominous inroads. A rule of thumb holds that bipolar disorder often emerges in late adolescence, whereas I was thirty-two at the time, and a family man with an advanced degree, so it's not surprising that my diagnosis was reliably established only five years later.

Serious mental illnesses often don't develop as textbooks and diagnostic manuals say they should. I'm a prime example of how supposedly established formulas quite often fail badly. My first episode of the illness, a severe depression, is the one I remember in great detail. This memoir is therefore slightly biased: my first mood swing is elaborated upon more than my fourteen or so hospitalizations.

After my first episode of insomnia, my family and I spent a few days touring Tel Aviv and Jaffa. Though pleased to be showing that part of the country to my wife, I began, unexpectedly, to ruminate about our finances. There was a kernel of reality in those worries: wc had savings of about five thousand dollars, and my panicky calculations convinced me that we needed five times more money to settle down in the Tel Aviv area comfortably. In the past I had never worried about money, but already in the first days of my illness I began suffering from what would soon become torturous symptoms: an almost incessant dread of penury, and the conviction that my plight was insoluble, no matter how hard I tried. In a few days I convinced myself that I had been condemned to live in abject hardship. Looking back, I can convincingly assert that my delusions of poverty were blown out of proportion. I had a relatively well-paying profession and could have easily increased my income by seeing private patients after hours. Kerstin was a professional librarian, and when our young son entered daycare, she could also work and bring home a paycheque. But already then my ruminations were shaping all of my thoughts and perceptions; it didn't even occur to me to share my fears and worries with Kerstin, or with close friends. I didn't explore whether I was thinking rationally or was in the throes of delusions.

My thinking in those days oscillated between the little I did own and some amount I would never achieve. And the more I obsessed about money, the more my problems grew and eventually took over. To make matters worse, since I saw no solutions to my plight, my future life was a series of endlessly recurring agonies, such as my family living in a crowded, scuzzy apartment. I felt deathly guilty for bringing my wife and children to Israel, when I was so poorly equipped to take care of them.

I blamed my absorption with literature and creative writing for my plight, and felt I was nothing but a callow daydreamer and an irresponsibly poor provider. In a matter of days my self-esteem had plummeted: instead of experiencing myself as a relatively competent young psychologist, I began to feel inadequate and unable to let go of my obsessions. Words like "failure," "stupid," or "selfish" began ringing in my ears, the first signs of the utter despair that would frequently assail me.

In a few days I began to experience some dominant traits of my illness, such as shifts in mood, flashes of panic, and painful worries, not to speak of the visceral conviction that my condition would never improve. A sense of helplessness, the leitmotif running through all my depressions, paid me tormenting visits. Instead of struggling, I felt hopelessly defeated, though the war hadn't even started. Vivid scenarios of wretchedness and suffering kept me awake in bed for hours.

The weekend arrived and I decided that come Sunday—Israel's first workday of the week—I would make arrangements to start working. That decision perked me up, and I worried significantly less about money. I called Shalvatah, the teaching hospital that had promised me a job in writing, and asked for the clinical director, Professor Harari. Her secretary gave me an appointment in three days. For several nights I slept better, as the prospect of soon resuming work infused me with courage, confident that my work at the hospital would somehow put an end to my worries. I recalled my internship in Kansas City, where my supervisors amply encouraged me, and it reassured me that I had what it took to do well in a new job. Memories of my pioneering work with groups of schizophrenics reinstated my belief of having quite a lot to offer.

PROFESSOR HARARI, AN ELDERLY WOMAN WITH WHITE, cropped hair, sat behind a small desk covered with books and patients' charts. She wore a white lab coat, what I considered the proper attire for internists or surgeons but not for a psychiatrist. She gauged me up and down, as if I were a slave on display before potential buyers. She listened intently, often turning her head to the side, apparently to hear me better. Or was it a tic?

As I found out later, she had never been married, having devoted her life to research and training in psychiatry and psychoanalysis. Quite formally she and I talked about hospital treatment of schizophrenics, and she asked me about my work in the States. Confident, if not cocky, I peered straight into her brown eyes. "I trained nurses to lead therapy groups," I explained. "I gave lectures and demonstrations, and used role playing to highlight thorny issues in practice and in theory."

She lifted her chin and gazed at me with cold, rock-hard eyes. "Do you have *data*, research evidence showing that the training made a difference?"

Data? I considered myself a trailblazer, an inventor of new methods, new techniques, and new vistas. I said to myself that research evidence was the department of dispassionate and punctilious researchers, rather unimaginative clods. Though her challenging me made me feel deflated, I inwardly told myself to be assertive. I peered into her eyes and said, "At this point in time, the only data I have is the nurses' confidence in leading therapy groups. They prefer this kind of work, rather than the traditional role of psychiatric nurse."

"And do you want to do this kind of work here? In Shalvatah?" She sounded more amused than peeved. "This is a small hospital, Doctor Camenietzki, not the behemoth you worked in, in the United States. You'd have to go slow, because the nurses here love what you called the 'traditional role.'"

I told myself I couldn't expect much support from Professor Harari because she clung to traditional roles, such as wearing a lab coat. "I know something that did work well for me," I declared. "I made the head nurse part and parcel of the training and the new role. If the boss goes along," I said, surprisingly alert, "the changes are more easily accepted."

She bent forward. "You're quite a charmer, Doctor Camenietzki! You flirt with the head nurse in hopes she'll help you introduce the changes you favour."

I felt I was blushing. It occurred to me to assert that the goal of supplying effective group therapy to dozens of patients justified the means, but a wave of fatigue came over me. "I don't see myself as a seducer, Doctor Harari," I mumbled apologetically, "just a psychologist intent on introducing much-needed changes."

"Relax, doctor," she said, at once imperious and light-hearted. "I'm an old pro, and loose metaphors frequently enter my mind." A ghost of a smile passed her lips. "Can you live with it?"

I straightened up my spine and said, "It looks like I've no choice in the matter. I've no control over the way you address your staff."

Her condescending smile now made me feel patronized. She pushed her chair back, stood up, and said, "Now, now, young man! No need to get uptight. I'll be glad to have you work for me." She put forth her hand. "Welcome on board!"

FOLLOWING MY INTERVIEW WITH PROFESSOR HARARI, I slept better for a few nights, but my worrying about money got worse. Daily I inflicted tortures and contempt on myself for returning to Israel with too little money. In my nine years as a student I paid no heed to financial matters, so absorbed was I with my studies and literary aspirations. But now that I was to provide for my family, material things loomed all-important and determined my happiness, self-esteem, and pride.

I saw no way out since gradual solutions, such as settling down slowly, didn't even occur to me. And it didn't enter my mind to ask my relatives for financial help, a common pattern in a country where relatives chip in to help struggling young couples. Kerstin was not pressuring me in any way, but my sleeplessness and noticeable anguish alarmed her. For years I had told her that I wished to live in Israel, but once there, I called all Israelis crass, greedy, and narrow-minded.

To make matters worse, my job at the hospital wasn't materializing. The Israeli red tape was causing me unrelenting fears and worries. My repeated calls to Shalvatah made it clear that my job had to be officially approved; Professor Harari's wish to hire me wasn't sufficient, since the hospital budget had to be updated. All that took time, a lot of time, as I was warned again and again. Weeks passed, I wasn't working, and had no means to move out of my parent's home and into my own apartment. Those obstacles made my venomous self-blame worse. One morning, Kerstin, our boys, and I took a long walk, an attempt to salve my free-flowing anxiety. We returned before noon, so I called the hospital to find out whether my job had been approved. The secretary sounded brusque, and when I timidly asked what was the matter, she replied that my mother had already called the hospital earlier that morning. "I don't understand why you are calling two hours after your mother," she blared out gruffly, in the typically Israeli way of overasserting oneself.

I was at once stunned and deathly embarrassed. Here I was, a thirty-two-year-old man, the head of a family with a PhD under my belt—and my mother calling my employer? I could hardly believe it! But instead of expressing anger, I became even more worried. What would happen now that it had become known in the hospital that I was a henpecked little boy? And what would Professor Harari think of me?

I stepped into the kitchen, where my mother was smoking a cigarette while washing dishes, as was her habit. She had her back to me, and somehow, inexplicably, I felt incapable of challenging her. Instead, I said meekly, "Please don't ever call the hospital again, Imma. It makes me look like a child incapable of taking care of himself." So castrated did I feel in the early days of my illness that I couldn't possibly confront my mother.

I had always been a reasonably assertive person who told others what he thought and how he felt. My recent wretchedness had changed me; I felt like a child scared of calling his meddlesome *yiddishe mamme* to account.

"Imma," I finally uttered, "the hospital secretary let me know that you called her this morning."

"Yes!" she exclaimed, without turning around. "I'm pretty angry that they're so slow to process your papers. Just as bureaucratic as a *shtetl*, in Poland!"

"But Imma," I replied, wholly dissatisfied with my soft, supplicant voice, "please don't call the hospital. It embarrasses me terribly." Down to my bones I was very cognizant of my dread of rocking the boat, because I believed a calamity would befall her and myself if I stood up to her.

She turned around, her cigarette now wedged between two wet fingers. "And what's wrong about a mother calling to ask about her son's situation?"

Her lack of empathy and insight floored me. Staring at her cigarette's billowing smoke, I timorously muttered, "But Imma, I'm not a nine-year-old."

"You're my son, and I'm upset that you're losing sleep over your job," she retorted. "I couldn't stop myself." She paused, trolling for correct, precise words. "Parents are forever, Shoolemshee, as you will learn from raising your children." Her cigarette now wedged between her lips, she said, "It breaks my heart to see you so depressed!"

Astonished, nearly overwhelmed, I made a supreme effort and asked, "Depressed? Why did you call me 'depressed,' Imma?"

"That's the way you come across, son. You rarely look me in the eye; you look as tormented as if you carried the entire world on your shoulders."

Being told that I looked depressed hit me hard. The night before I had attended a party at the home of Aaron, a childhood friend. It was a busy event with dozens of people chatting over drinks. The air was abuzz with laughter and loud conversation, but I felt acutely worried about others discerning how tormented I felt inside.

In a while, Aaron came up to Kerstin and spoke to her. He invited us to go with him and Kiki, his wife, to an eatery in Jaffa that featured excellent hummus and juicy shish kebab. I tried to listen and smile, but Aaron soon took me aside. "You look down," he said, "very down."

"I'm not aware of that," I commented self-effacingly.

The gap between Aaron's thick eyebrows had narrowed. "What's bothering you, my friend?"

"No news from the hospital. I'm living with my parents, and it's stressful. You know, Kerstin feels hemmed in at my mother's apartment."

"Yes, it will be better when she has her own place. But you really look down, Shalom."

"To be honest," I cried out, "what I feel is a lot of anguish and worries, not depression. It's not easy to resettle in Israel. Everything is so expensive, and somehow I feel I'm expected to live as comfortably as in the days I was living abroad."

Aaron nodded. "No doubt Israel has changed a lot in the last few years. The old pioneer frugality is a thing of the past." He looked around the room. "Sorry, I have to mix with other guests." He patted my upper arm. "Take care. Believe me, buddy, your bad mood is showing." That two people who knew me well had said I looked down in the dumps devastated me. How would I be able to work? How could I possibly maintain a calm and therapeutic relationship with my patients? I felt defeated, hopeless, and lonely.

After those exchanges with my mother and Aaron, I decided I couldn't go through life with a perpetual long face. I was committed to a career of assessing and treating people, so I vowed to cover up all of my suffering by wearing a "mask of sanity," as one theorist had called it.

After weeks of panicky waiting, at long last I was told over the phone that I could start working at the hospital. Unlike the sprawling buildings and vast lawns of Topeka State Hospital, Shalvatah consisted of a two-storey building, a few bungalows, and a tiny garden. I was not assigned an office of my own. "Your office will come later," Professor Harari told me on my first day on the job.

"But what about the patients?" I managed to challenge her. "They may find it odd that I see them in different offices without a permanent workplace."

"You are not in the States, doctor!"—Professor Harari never dropped my title—"And neither patients nor staff are spoiled. Private offices are symbols, not necessities!"

"Don't my patients need stability?" I asked, her irritating, know-it-all attitude propelling me to stand up to her. "*You*!" she blurted out. "You are the stability they need! The rest is just props! Changes in a therapist's office isn't what stops people from getting better! Never underestimate your patients' knee-jerk resistance to therapy!"

Professor Harari never passed up an opportunity to be didactic; she was never on a level with her staff. From heads of department to lowly medical students and psychologists, we all were her pupils in perpetuity. No one ever graduated.

On my first day at work, I met Dr. Naomi Matalon, my department head. She was a squat, busty woman of about forty-five, whose freckles accentuated her slightly puffy cheeks and attractive chestnut-brown eyes. Like all staff at Shalvatah, she wore a white lab coat while at the hospital. Every morning, Naomi made the rounds of her department, with eight of us in tow. The encounters with inpatients were quite blunt: diagnoses, prognoses, and treatments were openly discussed in the patients' presence; no one seemed to care whether or not the patients overheard the intimacies the staff openly discussed. Though Naomi fostered open communication with her staff, there was never any doubt about who made the difficult decisions and was the ultimate source of clinical wisdom. Though she paid close attention to the findings of psychological testing, her diagnoses and recommendations were not to be questioned, as she never failed to assert her authority. She appreciated my previous experience with psychotics and appointed me doctor in charge of a number of inpatients. At the time, in Israel, it was an innovation to have a psychologist in charge of hospitalized people.

Initially, Naomi's overall approach to patients under her care intrigued me in no small measure, so markedly did it differ from what I'd been taught in the United States. There was much use of shock treatments, and patients were quite frequently confined to isolation cells. Inpatients, as a rule, were treated as uninformed people whose feelings and conduct had to be monitored by mavens—myself one of them.

Once, as I fussed about having a woman's written authorization for me to obtain a report on her from another hospital, Naomi smiled amusedly. "She's a patient, *your* patient, isn't she?" She was alluding to my being an expert, and thus knowing what was best for a patient under my care. Thus, there was no need to fuss over rituals and formalities like patients' privacy and confidentiality.

I did learn a great deal from Naomi and her practices. Though a psychoanalyst in her private practice in the afternoon, at the hospital she was a biologically inclined psychiatrist who regarded psychotic illnesses as biological defects. She experienced no dissonance between the roles of psychoanalyst and biologically oriented psychiatrist, as she transitioned from one stance to another seamlessly and effortlessly.

Professor Harari's distinguishing between biological and psychoanalytic stances was even keener. Once, as I was strolling by the hospital's little garden, she stopped me. "Doctor Camenietzki," she exclaimed. "It came to my attention that twice a week you're engaging a group of schizophrenics in nonverbal warm-ups and exercises. This I think I understand. What I *don't* understand is your spending a whole hour discussing the meaning of group experiences after each session! What in God's name is there to discuss at such great length with outright sick people?"

She paused. "I'm not telling you to stop your experimentations, doctor, but be aware of your rosy, overoptimistic, Americanized approach! It's disrespectful when a doctor prettifies the hurt and pain caused by crippling disease processes."

Suddenly, I felt like opening up and sharing with Professor Harari the harrowing distress I was experiencing. Instantaneously, I decided never to do it because I believed she wouldn't show any empathy. I dreaded her suspending my work at the hospital until I had fully recovered from my depression and almost unceasing anxiety.

After a month of working at Shalvatah, my distress receded considerably; the reports I wrote and the treatments I performed were quite good. I became thoroughly involved in my work, and I paid close attention to practices and theories I had hitherto not been exposed to. Also, Kerstin and I had moved to our own apartment in Tel Aviv, and I felt relieved that now we had, at long last, a place of our own. Our three-year-old Martin entered a kindergarten, and twice a week my wife studied Hebrew in the evenings.

At the time, I had no doubts whatsoever that my suffering stemmed from my difficulties in readjusting to life in Israel. This was part and parcel of the sixties zeitgeist that viewed almost all experiences as something acquired, nurture rather than nature. Only five years later, when I was reliably diagnosed, did it dawn on me that my depression in Israel had been an endogenous process: plainly put, my condition couldn't be satisfactorily accounted for by external stresses and circumstances. I was, it turned out later, plagued by an inexorable psychiatric illness; the hardships involved in settling down in Israel duped me into thinking that I was reacting to life stresses. Despite my efforts to lead a "normal" life, my condition worsened, to the point that quite often I hurried home after work to take a nap, so as to forget my crippling sense of discouragement. Kerstin, who knew me as a consummate go-getter in graduate school and as a competitive young psychologist, was puzzled and alarmed. Like me, she attributed my growing despondence to the stress I was experiencing. She made sure, though, that our family was leading a predictable life. She warmly cared for our children, cooked and cleaned, and rarely complained about the small, furnished apartment we had rented. We soon learned that cockroaches would frantically scramble to hide whenever we switched on the kitchen's ceiling lights.

As I grew more dysfunctional by the day, I decided to seek therapy. The first therapist I thought of was Dr. Georges Tamarin, a psychologist who had taught a course on psychological testing at Tel Aviv University. While studying abroad, I had visited him at his home during a holiday in Israel. By then he was a well-known figure, as he had taken Tel Aviv University to court for firing him. The conflict revolved around his research on books in the Bible, especially Joshua, which he characterized as a textbook on the practice of genocide, and thus unfit for children. Dr. Tamarin vigorously mobilized European academics who protested the action taken against him.

We spent a long while discussing Dr. Tamarin's latest research on "The Israeli Schizophrenia." He maintained that, when the country was at peace, the typical Israeli wouldn't hesitate to backstab his fellow countrymen, to rake in a dollar or two. But when wars broke out, even egregious backstabbers would crawl under heavy machine-gun fire not to leave behind a wounded or dead Israeli soldier.

I mildly objected to Dr. Tamarin making use of a diagnostic concept to describe social and cultural processes, and he gazed at me piercingly, his eyes informing me that I might have been a good student but had a lot to learn still. We drank tea, but soon he volunteered that some of his thinking had been fashioned by his psychoanalysis in Yugoslavia during the Second World War. Both he and his Jewish analyst spent entire days doing nothing but reading and hiding from the Gestapo. "It was a good idea," Dr. Tamarin said, "for me to undergo an analysis, an opportunity for analyst and patient to spend some of their time meaningfully." I said to myself that North American psychoanalysts would dismiss such an undertaking as a bizarre venture. I said nothing, since I felt he'd shared with me a personal experience and it would have been wrong to invalidate his years-long therapy.

In 1971, when I approached him with a view to undergo psychotherapy, he responded that I already knew him well and it would be more effective if I had treatment with someone else. He recommended a few psychologists. I wholeheartedly thanked him but insisted on having him as my therapist because he would be unorthodox enough to understand that I was considering leaving Israel and returning to the United States. He wouldn't, I trusted, impose on me considerations such as staying in Israel to take care of my aging parents. As I uttered those words, I felt an icy needle travelling down my spine: for the first time I had mentioned myself leaving Israel, and its implications perplexed me. Only months before, the idea of *not* living in Israel was anathema to me. I must have looked shaken because we spent considerable time exploring my feelings about the issues I had just expressed.

We agreed on me starting therapy in a week. He said he would charge me what I charged my private patients. I replied I had none, since I felt too demoralized to treat anyone after a harrowing day's work at the hospital. His dark brown eyes gazed at me intensely, as if he'd grasped something essential about me.

He leaned forward and said, "Tell Naomi Matalon you are looking for work. Seeing patients in the late afternoon will help you to cope with helplessness." It was the first time ever I'd heard the word "helplessness" used in connection with my experiences; at once surprised and worried, I asked myself: Am I *that* bad off?

By way of replying, I implored, "I can barely do my work at the hospital. I don't think I could perform well in the late afternoon."

"Precisely because you claim you can't do extra work, you ought to give it a really good try," he said cuttingly. "Your finances are precarious, you told me. Some extra coin in your pocket will perk you up and enhance your self-esteem."

"I swear I can't," I kvetched.

"Let's deal with it next week, in your therapy session," his voice trailed off, an indication of the session being over.

A week later, a *khamsin* was on—a hot, dry, suffocating wind blowing from the desert that turned faces crimson and flared tempers. The shades in Dr. Tamarin's consulting room were drawn—like in all of Israel, I thought—and it was dark and gloomy. Close to the window there was a beat-up leather couch. He gazed at me quizzically, apparently expecting me to behave in a certain way. I had no idea what he wanted me to do or say.

"My fears and worries are getting worse," I lamented. "In the evenings, after dinner, I feel awfully down and discouraged."

He didn't reply. Instead, his hand invitingly gestured toward his decrepit couch.

I was flabbergasted. Couch? I had no interest whatsoever in psychoanalysis. I wanted, first and foremost, to talk and talk about how miserable I felt. For a while I studied the couch, then turned to him. "I'm not ready for a couch," I said. "As a matter of fact, I don't think I need it."

He raised his eyebrows and kept them up. "How is it that you, a psychologist, show such blatant resistance to therapy? You damn well know what's expected of you," he angrily raised his voice. "Just lie on the couch, stare at the ceiling, and start talking!"

His directness and imperious voice, so different from the "warmth and empathy" drilled into me in graduate school, intimidated me. And yet I knew he wasn't much off target. I wanted to discuss my unceasing suffering, but analyzing its lurking causes was not on my agenda, since I believed I was responding to obvious stresses. Amazed at his confrontational style, I slowly stood up, doddered toward the couch, and lay on it, silent. I justified my compliance by telling myself, "Dr. Tamarin is a therapist of the old school. He'll emphasize my resistance to therapy and pay close attention to our evolving relationship."

I spent the rest of the session elaborating on how I regarded him highly, the only reason for me to comply with the treatment he had in mind. He voiced a few monosyllables, and chain-smoked while I talked. Soon I lit my own cigarette, hoping he would tell me not to smoke, an injunction I was determined to disobey. He didn't, however, utter a word about my smoking, and I felt cheated out of a fight I had been looking forward to.

In the next few sessions I wailed and whined, feeling terribly sorry for myself as I lamented my lousy moods getting worse. Once, he interrupted me right in the middle of a string of self-pitying complaints: "You came back to Israel," he vigorously declared, "not to be a writer or a psychologist, but to be pampered by your mother!"

His interpretation stunned me. First, it astonished me that he, evidently, hadn't been listening to my complaints about my worsening condition. I took my time and in my mind reviewed my relationship with my mother, from infancy on. Then I muttered to myself, "Throughout, there was very little about my mother that was warm and cuddly. She did try to be loving and demonstrative, but I often felt that we were miles apart from one another."

I raised my voice as I asked, "Did you say *pampered* by my mother, Dr. Tamarin? Of all people?" My own directness surprised me, as I added, "Excuse me, doctor, but that's nonsense, an oxymoron no better than 'lukewarm iceberg!'"

After a pause, I continued, "Dr. Tamarin, your theory leaves me cold, just as my mother's chill has been frustrating me as far back as I remember!" But out of loyalty to a mentor I deemed admirable, I asked myself, Am I that deprived inside? Have I been deluding myself that becoming a recognized writer would somehow compensate me for a lifelong emotional privation?

Looking back on Dr. Tamarin's brutal intervention, I realize that unconscious motivations of mine had been pointed out, and their implications were hurting me immensely. I spent the next therapy sessions discussing the impact of his assault on me, and how shocked and frightened his interpretation had made me feel. But soon I went back to lamenting my escalating suffering, so that neither he nor I ever again mentioned wishes to be spoiled by my tepid mother.

As I wouldn't stop complaining about my unrelenting suffering, my therapist would challenge my passivity and demoralization. Evidently, he feared that my sense of helplessness was becoming ingrained, a second nature of sorts. Since he never suspected that mine was an endogenous depression, his interventions aimed at reframing my sense of doom and despair and helping me to think constructively of my life and myself.

Only years after I stopped seeing Dr. Tamarin did I become aware of cognitive therapy and its emphasis on how people think and process information, and what core beliefs they hold on to. I'm convinced that he went to his grave without ever hearing of it. I'm positive, though, that he would have admitted that correcting my distorted thinking was the most important item on his agenda.

Dr. Tamarin, like all experienced clinicians, relied on his intuition much more than on any theories and established practices. He did, however, change tactics once he realized that interpreting the presumably unconscious causes of my problems did not benefit me at all. Throughout, he sounded impatient and gruff over my almost ceaseless kvetching, since it never occurred to him that mine was an alarming psychotic illness. As I displayed no pathologically elevated moods while in therapy with him, it was, as mentioned, impossible to conclude that a bipolar disorder was to blame for my worsening depression.

Apparently frustrated by the lack of progress in my therapy, Dr. Tamarin referred me to a psychiatrist who would prescribe medication. Unfortunately, the old antidepressants had no therapeutic impact on me, but didn't cause crippling side effects either. Like my therapist, that psychiatrist assumed I was overreacting to life stresses.

In the last four decades, I've never blamed Dr. Tamarin, other clinicians, or myself for failing to grasp the underlying nature of my disorder.

Meanwhile, life at home was deteriorating. Six days a week I woke up early and hurried to the hospital. A few afternoons a week I was busy with my private practice of psychotherapy. Kerstin couldn't understand what was wrong with me. For years I'd been lecturing her that we would live in Israel, and that Hebrew was the language in which I would write short stories and novels. And yet, shortly after returning to Israel, I collapsed like a house of cards, and I wondered where all my resilience had gone.

Surprisingly, my work as a therapist was coming along reasonably well, a baffling phenomenon since I was often convinced I was a worthless clinician. I couldn't believe my ears when the father of a schizophrenic young man profusely thanked Naomi Matalon for referring his son to me. Both my patient and his father reported that he was making good progress after seeing me for only three months. It floored me that people regarded me as a competent psychologist, since it vindicated Dr. Tamarin's stance that my supposed incompetence was nothing but a distortion.

My ability to conduct acceptable therapy, even while verging on a psychosis, became clear to me only years later.

I came to realize that the role of psychotherapist is one of the most protected roles on earth. A well-trained therapist can effectively conceal almost any flaw and dysfunction of his own. This happens because psychotherapists reveal only what's perfectly safe to divulge, like skipping classes in grade nine, or being turned on by one's sexy-looking grade-ten English teacher. Psychologists, for instance, are thoroughly trained to deal with crises, such as patients blaming the doctor for lack of progress. The mystique is further enhanced by therapists being socially sanctioned mavens on managing subtle feelings and relationships.

Despite my bipolar disorder, in the five decades that I worked as a psychologist, only two patients of mine ever found out that I was in the throes of severe mental illness. Later I'll elaborate on how their "discovery" came about.

At Shalvatah, staff had lunch in the hospital cafeteria. As my condition worsened, I would sit by myself to avoid contact with my co-workers. Pleasant small talk with colleagues felt like an obstacle course I could never complete. I felt inadequate listening to my co-workers' chit-chat about movies they had seen or books they were reading. I rarely took my wife to the movies, and my concentration was so impaired that I managed to read only newspapers.

Feeling defeated, one day after lunch I headed from the cafeteria to the secretary's office. In a whisper I let her know that I wasn't well—"a flu of sorts"—and was heading home. Never before had I succumbed to my nasty moods while at work. My capitulation made me feel worse, and I vowed never to repeat that mistake.

I've since then been abiding by a simple theory: a single admission of defeat might lead to admitting other defeats, and soon I'd be giving up the entire struggle for survival.

Chapter 2

Hell on Earth Gets Worse

FOUR MONTHS AFTER ARRIVING IN ISRAEL, Kerstin and I celebrated our fourth wedding anniversary in a fine restaurant. We entrusted, for the first time ever, a babysitter with our two sons, one of them a baby, the other one a toddler. We planned on having a really good time.

Truth was, intense suicidal thoughts had begun assailing me days before our anniversary. Initially, they came over me whenever I reflected on how loathsome my life had become, but soon they occurred unexpectedly, almost at random. I began to daydream of jumping to my death from a tall building, overdosing on painkillers, or jumping in front of a speeding truck. Those daydreams eventually coalesced into a vivid fantasy of shooting myself in the head. In Israel, I saw weapons everywhere, and I envied young soldiers lugging their rifles; guns epitomized the freedom to end my ordeals. I tried hard to obviate these obsessions, but they assailed me when I was off work and my mind was free to wander.

At the restaurant, I endeavoured to engage my wife in a romantic, light-hearted conversation on how we had first met at a Fourth of July dance in Kansas. But soon she was doing most of the talking, and I struggled to maintain acceptable eye contact with her.

"You look worried," Kerstin said after a pause in the conversation.

"I was thinking about work," I lied. Once again I had been considering the details of shooting myself. I imagined myself snatching a rifle off a young soldier, cocking it, shoving the muzzle into my mouth, and pulling the trigger. But all I was actually doing was composing, writing, and rewriting mad, fleeting scenarios of death by suicide.

"Can't you share with me what you're thinking?" My wife smiled coyly.

It would take decades before I shared with my wife my immensely disturbing daydreams of taking my own life. I kept silent for fear of frightening her, since there was little she could do to help me, I thought. There is, I maintain, something altruistic about the suicidal person who keeps his suicidal thoughts to himself. But such concealment soon becomes self-destructive: if friends and families are not aware of one's suicidal ruminations, they cannot, for example, drive you to the nearest hospital or contact a health-care professional.

Before I could reassure my wife, the waiter served the main course. We tasted and commented on our choices, and for a short while the conversation flowed. But soon it died out, and after we had silently stared at each other, I broke the silence. "Kerstin," I whispered, gazing at her left earring, "I'm thinking of returning to the States."

Utterly bewildered, she set her fork and knife beside her plate. "Ever since I met you, Israel was said to be your home. You insisted on living here."

"I know, I know," I nodded, "but all my plans have woefully failed. We're broke, we can't afford an apartment to our taste, and I'm depressed out of my head. I want out!"

My wife looked about worriedly, checking whether people nearby had heard my outburst. "But what about your wishes to be a writer?" she asked.

I shook my head. "They were nothing but daydreams! Truth is, I have failed as a provider. It would take me many years to feel I belong in modern Israel. As my friend Aaron said, the Six Day War changed Israel inalterably, and I don't wish to be part of it. I long for the easy life we had in the United States."

For a while she was quiet, then bent forward, "What about your parents?"

I placed my palms on my cheeks. "They will suffer—a lot, I think—but I really want to resume the life we had before I became so...so...dysfunctional, so ashamed...of myself." I deliberately didn't mention terms like "depression" or "anxiety," for fear of getting carried away and admitting to thoughts of ending my life.

"Eat your chicken," my wife urged me. "It's getting cold."

"Tomorrow," I proclaimed, "I'll be writing Topeka State Hospital to see if they have a job for me, and if they can speed up our immigration visas."

"Aren't you in a terrible hurry?" Kerstin held my hand. "We've been in Tel Aviv four months, and you're giving up already? Give yourself time to think it over."

I felt like yelling that I was a volcano about to erupt, and that I would likely end up killing myself unless I made drastic changes to my life. Gazing at my perplexed wife made me feel so inadequate that even killing myself seemed beyond my capacity to take action. To calm her, I picked at the food on my plate, though my appetite had completely vanished.

Sleep disturbances are almost ubiquitous features of clinical depressions, with most patients sleeping too little, others too much, and still others dozing on and off due to chronic sleep deprivation. My problem was not falling asleep but waking up early, thus sleeping, on average, five hours a night.

Mentally ill people are not in this world to entertain their therapists. Yet some of us are hard to listen to, as we drone on and on about our troubles. A case in point was Rivka, a thirty-something woman admitted to Shalvatah after outpatient therapies had failed to help her. My colleagues were of the unanimous opinion that she was in the throes of "erotomania." Indeed, she harboured intense fantasies that men, young and old, were irresistibly attracted to her, that they would fall in love with her and insist on having "raunchy sex" with her.

Before entering the hospital, her condition had worsened. She began accusing total strangers on buses and on the street of attempting to seduce her. Young men were accused of making suggestive and lewd gestures; she protected herself by loudly unmasking their perfidy, as she put it. She had been fired from several jobs, and things got even worse when she began assaulting male relatives or calling their wives to reveal their husbands' designs on her.

These days, she would be diagnosed as ailing from a delusional disorder and prescribed antipsychotic medication. Four decades ago, however, medications were less curative than nowadays, and psychotherapy loomed as the only treatment available to Rivka. When Naomi Matalon referred her to me, she emphatically wished me good luck; her pessimism sounded as clear as church bells ringing.

Rivka was tall and slim. She rarely combed her curly dark brown hair. Her thick, black-framed eyeglasses were markedly old-fashioned and often slid down her nose. She wore no makeup, and at all times looked tired. Her loose, not always clean, clothes suggested neglect, and I asked the nurses to make sure she showered daily and wore clean clothes. Before long I realized that she put no effort into looking presentable, since all men lusted for her anyhow.

I began seeing her several times a week, and she initially intrigued me. After four sessions, however, I knew all about her delusions and could predict when outbursts of rage would occur. By the tenth session I was growing impatient, since all my attempts to inculcate insights fell by the wayside. She behaved as if she hadn't at all heard my suggestions. All my attempts to explore her underlying loneliness failed completely.

One day, at the peak of my sleep disorder, an awful *khamsin* was blowing. Air conditioning was rare in those days, and people stayed indoors with the shutters closed. I sleepily listened to Rivka's repetitious droning about the amorous but dangerous men in her life. A huge fly buzzed almost nonstop in the room, desperately banging against the windowpanes and enhancing my sense of desolation prompted by the unendurable heat and Rivka's fretful whimpering. I stifled yawn after yawn, and racked my brain as I searched for an interpretation that would put an end to her accusations. Tears filled my eyes, and I closed them—for just one second, I told myself.

I came to with a start, and all at once the scene made sense: the gloom, the droning fan, the buzzing fly, my perspiring face. I felt painfully alert and noticed droplets glimmering on Rivka's forehead. She was peering at me intensely.

"I'm very sorry," I murmured, deathly embarrassed. "The heat got to me. Please, go on."

She gazed at me, now looking perplexed. Fury? I asked myself. Disillusionment? Disgust?

"How do you really feel, Rivka?" I asked sheepishly. "It's true that I dozed off while you were talking, but what's your gut reaction? Please tell me. I want to know! I need to know!"

Somehow, I wished I could confide in her and confess that for months I had been sleeping poorly, but Rivka vetted me coldly, her eyes bespeaking visceral disgust. Not in a million years would she have felt compassion for my plight. She peered at me, as though I were covered with shit.

"Please don't keep me in suspense, Rivka," I raised my voice. "Tell me, how do you feel about me falling asleep?"

She inhaled deeply, slowly pushed back her screechy chair, and rose to her feet. Without a word, she turned around, waddled to the door, and opened it. It felt like the hellish heat outside would incinerate me. Her silence was the worst punishment she could inflict on me. Next morning she informed me she'd decided to sign herself out of the hospital. I indicated that my falling asleep must have hurt her; her ending therapy reflected furious disappointment with me. I felt guilty of the way I had treated Rivka, but Dr. Tamarin merely exclaimed, "You're not Superman! Failing to help difficult patients is not uncommon. Just think about people dying on operating tables! If surgeons, like you, felt guilty over patients they couldn't help, their careers would come to an end."

My work with Rivka was the first and last time that I fell asleep in front of a patient. Over the decades, my eyes fluttered when patients bored me, or when I was acutely sleep-deprived. I must at times have come across as aloof, perhaps even disinterested. Yes, I've occasionally been sleepy at work, and over the years a few patients poignantly confronted me. The memory of Rivka's silent repugnance is a ghost stricter than any professional code of ethics, more condemning than any real or imagined denunciations by my colleagues.

My suicidal obsessions radically changed my self-concept—the ways I thought of myself, that is. In the past, I considered myself a go-getter committed to enjoying a challenging, productive life. The advent of distorted thinking, such as my core belief of being hopelessly dysfunctional, changed my self-image: I took refuge in passivity and almost never modified my routines. Instead of experiencing myself as a person in pursuit of his goals, I felt just as useless as a car that had run out of fuel.

The unceasing impulses to destroy myself affected some of my deepest and most cherished beliefs. Ever since my studies in philosophy, first as an undergraduate, then in graduate school, I had been an ardent admirer of existentialism. Perhaps naively, I postulated that, even in intolerable situations, I would contemplate options, and then act on the choices I'd freely made. But once confronted with seemingly invincible suicidal ideations, philosophers' prescriptions on how to conduct my life looked awfully good on paper but soon disintegrated like a high-rise hit by a thousand-pound bomb. In particular, Sartre's notion that we humans "are condemned to be free" rankled me a great deal, since this implied I could choose how to live and how to die. Yes, I had some control over myself, like stopping breathing for a minute or two. But suicidal torments daily reinstated themselves and inside my head exploded like popcorn laid out on a red-hot iron tray.

Choices? What choices? What brought me relief were not actions inspired by lovely-sounding metaphysical speculations; what kept me alive were brutish self-preservation instincts, akin to a housefly's frantic struggles to survive a man hell-bent on swatting it dead.

Since ingrained beliefs don't readily vanish, it took me years to redefine my identity. Though in my personal life I believe that humans are endowed with free will, I rejected all facile speculations about innate freedom, as I realized how cold and simplistic those libertarian views were. I couldn't—still can't—conceive of something more insensitive than insisting that people just about to kill themselves are "free to make choices." Many early mornings, before I could tell a wolf from a dog, I'd ask myself, "Should I kill myself right now? Or perhaps tomorrow, after dinnertime?"

Philosophers are anything but stupid. They certainly know there are attributes we humans cannot choose, like our height or the colour of our irises. Those attributes are destiny, fate, or karma, which Heidegger and Sartre knew very well. But since they were scholars dying to be admired by fellow scholars, they wrote lengthy passages on psychotic-sounding neologisms like "thrownness" or "facticity." Their simple ideas could quite easily be explicated by bright undergraduate students, in a hundred words or less.

In days of black despair I self-loathingly regretted the thousands of hours I had spent reading abstruse, yet essentially simple, ideas about death awaiting all of us. Existentialism, and especially Sartre's notions of some ineluctable freedom, is nothing but a privilege of the symptom-free. And though Heidegger insisted he was no existentialist, his quest for the meaning of Being is a pastime for the mentally healthy, best enjoyed over a tumbler of cognac after dessert and coffee.

We madmen are crippled by odious symptoms some of the time; fortunately, medical research and advances in psychological therapies are slowly, very slowly, but without a break shrinking the "some of the time" that makes our wretched lives so goddamn painful.

THE WEEKS AND MONTHS AFTER I DECLARED MY INTENTION to leave Israel were some of the most distressing days of my life, as I felt I would be abandoning my aging parents. Waves of guilt began washing over me once I'd decided to fulfil my own needs, not my parents'. My older brother, a cardiologist in Brazil, had no intentions of ever living in Israel. Consequently, my parents had long accepted that he wouldn't be comforting them in their old age. Honouring my father and mother was a commandment I'd all my life been keenly aware of.

Dr. Tamarin assumed a nonjudgmental approach as he remarked, "These days your car happens to be parked right here, in Israel. Why don't you give it a try? See what's in it for you."

"But I'm falling apart, doctor," I gruffly riposted, feeling misunderstood and lonely. "If I stay in Israel, I'll end up killing myself!"

Had I known at the time that my condition was not a situational crisis of sorts but a severe mental illness I might not have left Israel. I would have stayed put and fought back my disorder, since it would have greatly troubled me, no matter where on the planet I chose to live. My entire life I have subscribed to the notion that bipolar disorder is a disease stemming from faulty biochemistry of the brain. Though the illness, like almost all ailments, is adversely affected by emotional setbacks or excessive stress, the brain dysfunction is unlikely to improve just because the patient moves far away from his current address. Many times I have cautioned people against "geographical solutions," such as moving from Toronto to Vancouver to evade one's inerasable fate.

By December 1971, my previous employers at Topeka State Hospital had written me that they were very happy to have me back. My application for immigrant visas to the United States was, however, mistakenly sent to Rio de Janeiro, my place of birth, not to the American consulate in Tel Aviv. It took months for the American authorities to correct their mistake, but once the visas arrived, I was prepared to resume my pre-morbid life in the States. But before I said goodbye to my parents, I had to overcome what I called, for lack of a better term, "my Siamese-twin attachment." It is an abstruse, quite delusional concept, a reflection of myself inching toward madness. In essence, I felt so guilty of "abandoning" my parents that my right hip felt like it was anatomically attached to theirs. At the time, I even felt that my right hip was physically protruding, but the more I attempted to talk myself out of that distortion, the larger and heavier the hipbone felt. Massaging my right side, to prove that I was no extension of my parents, soothed me temporarily, but the delusion would return in a few hours.

I obtained some relief by sharing with my parents and friends my reasons for returning to the United States. Shame and embarrassment flooded me when I confessed that my year-long stay in Israel had been a total failure. Not only hadn't I adapted to life's circumstances, but I had inflicted unnecessary pain on my wife, my parents, and my children.

Another obstacle was my realization that I'd better give up my daydreams of becoming a writer, a fantasy I had indulged in since my teens. It took me two decades before I felt reasonably confident and capable of writing fiction—in English, the language I spoke at work and at home.

While depressed, I suffered greatly on account of the lack of spontaneity and playfulness while dealing with my sons. After work at the hospital and treating private patients, all too often I spent the afternoon at home, taking a nap or just hiding in bed. My perplexed wife felt lonely and neglected as she struggled to survive in a country foreign to her with almost no support from her husband. One of her reliefs from chores was attending an *ulpan*, a school for those eager to learn Hebrew.

Kerstin toiled to maintain her sanity despite the children's multiple illnesses. It appeared that our boys had been cursed with every Levantine microbe and virus. Fever followed fever, and there seemed to be no end to their ailments. Kerstin herself caught some of these illnesses and lost considerable weight. Her family doctor summoned me to her office and told me, in typical Israeli abrasiveness, that since I wasn't spending enough time with my wife, I was the cause of her repeated ailments.

TO THIS DAY I'M STILL CONVINCED THAT MY SONS EXPErienced a great deal of suffering. I was neither warm nor available to them, and experienced difficulties spending "quality time" with them. A case in point was the huge black trunk in which we had shipped our belongings from Kansas to Tel Aviv. I decided not to get rid of that bulky item once I committed myself to returning to the States. Instead, it stood in the hallway at the entrance to our apartment, covered by a pink tablecloth and an African statuette. On rainy days, or when the heat outdoors was unbearable, I entertained my children with the trunk.

The games we played were simple. First, I removed the statuette and the tablecloth; then I sat at the head of the trunk and played truck driver. Hooting and tooting to keep myself alert, I would improvise variations, such as my children waiting for a bus to stop, or Martin, then three years old, loading the truck with toys. He easily caught on to this game, while Daniel, then about a year and a half old, rejoiced in the unceasing noises his brother and father were making. We also played taxicab, camel, or elephant—anything that could be driven or loaded with passengers and toys. My goal was to exuberate, be loud and boisterous. Martin would laugh with excitement, while baby Daniel joined the tumult by gesticulating, kicking his chubby legs, and trying hard to make noises.

But the revelry wouldn't last long. After minutes of ebullience, my enthusiasm would precipitously wane and seething despair would take over. Lethargic and my despair growing, I would ask Martin to play driver as I placed Daniel right behind him. I crouched by the rear of the imaginary truck or camel, my hands hiding my face and my eyes kept closed, to forget, for a moment, the depression currently devastating me.

Soon the boys' noise would irritate me, and I felt guilty for no longer playing with them. My guilt, however, didn't alter my behaviour. Rather, I crouched, half asleep and out of touch with my surroundings, until Martin got tired of playing driver. Eager to have fun, he would dismount the trunk, amble to the kitchen, and ask his mother to hand him a cookie. I felt worthless, and chastised myself harshly for my inability to provide the affection my children craved.

Saturday morning walks with my children proved equally disastrous. I wanted to relieve Kerstin from the intensive care of our boys by taking them to a nearby park. Pushing the baby stroller always gave me hope that this time around I would be playful with my sons for a whole hour. But after Martin had frolicked awhile in the sandbox or on the slides, what felt like ten-foot-high waves of melancholia came washing over me. Giddy and numb, I sat on a bench, paralyzed.

Martin played with other children and demanded nothing from me, probably sensing I was avoiding him. I would hold baby Daniel in my arms, briefly rocking and singing to him until a renewed bout of despondency immobilized me. I would then stand up and move about playfully, but those were acts born of desperation that never lasted long. No matter how hard I tried, I felt incapable of joining Martin's play or Daniel's happy purling and gurgling.

The growing alienation from my children stood in sharp contrast with my conduct prior to my first clinical depression. A creature of the sixties, I had done all I could to be a supportive husband and a caring father, such as helping to prepare dinners or energetically changing and rinsing diapers. The self-accusations of not playing spontaneously with my sons made me feel terribly sorry for them. I castigated myself for disrupting—irreparably, I thought—their quiet, happy, early life in Kansas, and miserably failing to be affectionate and demonstrative while we lived in Tel Aviv.

Kerstin was at all times very loving and caring, and she significantly reduced the impact of my neglect. But deep inside I felt I had damaged my sons for good. And the more I accused myself, the less I interacted with my children and the guiltier I felt. In those days, I was my own prosecutor, merciless judge, cold-hearted jury, and over-eager executioner all rolled into one.

By April 1972, a hard reality of living in Israel caught up with me when a letter notified me of a week of reserve military duty. From late 1958 till mid-1961, I had served in the artillery branch. Those were relatively quiet times between Israel and its neighbours; I participated in no combat, only in unending training and manoeuvres. After thirteen months, I became a corporal and an instructor of reservists. In the dying days of service, I was promoted to the rank of sergeant.

As a soldier I carried out whatever my superiors expected of me but was never pleased with life in the military. At times I did nothing for weeks, and, to spend time constructively, I studied French on my own. Following my discharge from active duty, I was assigned to the anti-aircraft corps, as I had been injured when a reservist fired a heavy mortar before being ordered to. I was inspecting the mortar's aiming device, and that accident caused me near-deafness for a month. Since then, I've been somewhat hard of hearing, a condition impossible to hide, so unlike my systematic concealment of mental illness.

Upon reading the letter advising me of my reserve duty, I became excruciatingly fearful—a predictable response whenever inevitable changes to my routines took place. Again and again I berated myself, "You'll fuck up royally!" as I worried about acting unmanly and appearing weak and incompetent.

During reserve duty, we were instructed on anti-aircraft defence, first aid, and management of dead and wounded civilians. Quite often I felt confused, as I was certain that my abysmal insecurity was affecting me physically and mentally. At night trainees would take turns standing guard at military installations. I remember that my turn to stand guard fell on a Thursday night, the night the troops were busy polishing their quarters and equipment for the Friday morning review. After the sergeant inspected us and our equipment, we were marched to a nearby military theatre, where *Love Story* was being screened.

From the start I couldn't follow the storyline, and feared that I'd somehow become the platoon's laughing stock. I gasped for air as the movie continued, and palpitations came over me. Out of the blue, a cruel voice inside me trumpeted, "You're dying! You're dying!" I imagined myself collapsing in the movie theatre and my fellow reservists carrying me to the infirmary. How embarrassing! Who had ever heard of a healthy thirty-three-year-old dying of a heart attack?

But the moment the term "heart attack" occurred to me, I began patting my wildly beating heart. I imagined myself lying on a bed in a military hospital, with my grim parents and wife watching me. I fantasized staying in bed for months, and my career coming to an end. And yet I was well aware of a panic attack gripping me.

Soon I began feeling like a fool. Though no one had noticed my upset, the inner commotion I'd created deathly embarrassed me. I looked about and saw that the soldiers to my left and to my right had their eyes riveted to the movie, their faces faintly aglow from the light emanating from the large screen. In the film, a hockey player was holding a good-looking young woman who was dying of cancer. So what are you fretting about? I chastened myself, since a genuine tragedy was unfolding before my eyes. By the end of the film I felt calmer, yet ashamed of the preposterous and undignified brouhaha I had inflicted on myself.

From the theatre, the platoon marched back to our barracks. My guard duty was from midnight to two a.m., and I had about two hours to sleep in the sentries' tent. I was, however, too restless to fall asleep, as I dreaded the recurrence of panic attacks.

I must have fallen asleep, because one of the guards on the ten-to-midnight watch shook me awake. I patted my web gear to confirm that I had ammunition with me, then held my rifle up as I muttered, "I'm ready," to inform my fellow guard that I was about to relieve him.

Moments later, I was patrolling the perimeter of a military supply depot, my rifle slung over my shoulder and its muzzle aiming at the hazy, starless skies. I listened to the distant whirring of cars and trucks on the Tel Aviv–Jerusalem highway and studied the overcast spring firmament, with a wide, pink halo above Tel Aviv. I had two hours to kill, but the memory of my panic attack discouraged me completely.

All at once it stunned me that I had with me a loaded rifle, with a bullet in the chamber and the safety off. I recalled months of ad nauseam fantasizing about a rifle's icy muzzle either poking my temple or stuffed into my mouth.

But, enigmatically, my weapon vindicated something profound and indefinable, yet impossible to ignore. And before I grasped whatever my own depths were telling me, I heard an inner voice nagging at me: "It's now or never, man! Never again will you be able to put an end to your miseries painlessly! You'll forever regret any postponement or indecision!" I slid the rifle off my shoulder, clutched it with both hands, and lovingly fondled the trigger guard. I only had to insert the muzzle into my mouth and squeeze the trigger. I pictured my skull shattering, and my brain slithering down my neck. I would collapse and morph into an inert, insentient carcass on the ground.

For a while I felt anxious because I hadn't left a good-bye note to my wife. I truly wanted to die, and penning a final note to my family was, in my eyes, nothing but an inconsequential convention.

But the thought of my children growing up without a father gave me pause, and I relaxed my forefinger resting on the trigger guard. Not only would they be orphans at an early age but they would live in Sweden, since Kerstin would no doubt move back to where she had been born and bred. Unexpectedly, I became thoroughly engrossed in the "Who is a Jew?" controversy. All my life I had been a totally irreligious person, but now I violently objected to my sons growing up in a country where the Lutheran church was the state religion.

After brief but intense soul-searching, I resolved to ensure that my children would one day embrace my entirely godless Judaism. I wanted them to grow up with no religion, no prayers, and no commandments lording it over every moment of their lives. Before long I felt an invigorating urge to share with Kerstin and Doctor Tamarin my "rediscovery" of the secular Jew in me.

Slowly, and cognizant of giving up my freedom to end my life, I removed the ammunition from my rifle to guarantee I wouldn't kill myself on a sudden impulse. I could be court-martialled for neglecting my sentry duty. And yet I was determined to give my pain-ridden life just one more try, however unsatisfactory it might turn out. In retrospect, caring for my children, and them becoming irreligious Jews, had temporarily triumphed over pathological urges to die by suicide.

My military duty over, I began to obsess about my visa to the United States. Friends at Topeka State Hospital had reassured me that all necessary steps had been taken, and the visas were now in the hands of the American consul in Tel Aviv. Phone calls to the consulate yielded no reassuring answers, and I frantically agonized over scenarios of never leaving Israel, never obtaining relief, never becoming a writer. The game of "never" something or another was a personal torment, since I had persuaded myself that my nightmarish fantasies were incontestable realities.

At that time I wasn't benefitting much from Dr. Tamarin's treatment. In retrospect, he probably had limited patience for my lamenting how excruciatingly painful my life was. He must have been frustrated because once, in an annoyed voice, he said, "You keep coming back to taking your life. Have you ever thought of your wife making love to another man?"

That confrontation amused me and I laughed heartily. Me? Jealous? From the grave? I was not a possessive husband and had never asked my wife about her sex life prior to meeting me. And in my regressed condition it was an utter waste of breath to bring up sexuality. Sex? For months I had experienced no arousal whatsoever, and having an erection was, to me, a factual impossibility.

As I write this memoir, I feel that Dr. Tamarin subjected me to confrontations aimed at shaking me out of passivity, lack of initiative, and helplessness. I respected and admired him, and forty years later I'm still grateful to him for keeping me alive. As a psychologist, I learned from his mistakes, and I avoid confrontations with vulnerable people. The latter need a calm, benevolent therapist that neither yields to their despair nor tries to talk them out of their feelings, however outrageous they may be. Unlike Dr. Tamarin, I minimize confrontations and urge my patients to live as pleasurably as their disorders allow. "The best antidepressant on the market," I preach impishly, "is having a beer and a pizza with a good friend, catching up, laughing, and having a good time for an hour or so."

Despite my self-inflicted upsets, our visas to the States finally arrived, and the doors were now wide open toward resuming my pre-morbid life. And yet I continued to sleep poorly, ate too little, worried too much, and devastating moods still disturbed me immensely. That alone should have been a warning: my depression was largely endogenous, since favourable changes in external circumstances didn't at all affect the way I felt.

Prior to leaving Israel, Kerstin urged me to change our children's first names. From birth until we left Israel, Martin was called Yishai, the Hebrew name for the Biblical Jesse, King David's father. Daniel was then called Yokhy, a diminutive for Yokhanan, the Hebrew source of the Anglo-Saxon John. I agreed with her since we would be living in North America, and hard-to-pronounce names could become unnecessary burdens.

During my final session with Dr. Tamarin, as I was sitting up and not lying on his couch, his face lit up as I told him of my wife and me changing our sons' first names. "It's a step in the right direction," he exclaimed, probably the only time I ever heard words of praise coming out of him. But before I could absorb this aspect of my therapist's personality, he added, "At the time, you made sure to give your sons Hebrew names because of your shallow chauvinism and daydreams of becoming an Israeli writer, in Hebrew. I'm glad to hear that this time around you didn't lord it over your wife and accepted her views and her needs."

I had then the distinct impression that he wanted to have the last word, as far as I was concerned, but I kept mum, because I wanted to thank him for all the help he had given me, and not carp about secondary issues, the way he was carrying on. It even entered my mind that he was having difficulty saying goodbye to a patient who not only admired him but voiced those feelings again and again.

Chapter 3

The Interlude

Back in Lawrence, Kansas, my wife and I once again were struck by that city's lack of charm. Its buildings looked dull and unappealing, except for a few old buildings on the University of Kansas campus. Restaurants served no wine or alcoholic beverages, and huge billboards proclaimed, "Denounce liquor by the ounce!" Movie theatres showed only Hollywood fare, never the foreign films my wife and I preferred. The proximity of Lawrence to the Menninger Clinic, then in Topeka, led me to observe that the only inspiring venues in Kansas were daily psychoanalysis on weekdays and church attendance on Sundays.

Still, our lives unfolded smoothly. I bought a new car, and we resumed our picnics in the countryside, something we hadn't done in Israel, since I felt too insecure and too helpless to rent a car and drive it. The apartment we rented, within walking distance from the university campus, was airy and pleasant, but once Kerstin resumed her work as a librarian, we moved into a more spacious townhouse. We lived comfortably, and I no longer worried about money. Thanks to my contacts in the psychology department, our children were admitted to a lovely experimental kindergarten on campus. My wife and I felt reassured and confident about the present, and we expected the good times to last.

I easily resumed work at Topeka State Hospital. I immediately decided to change the way I worked completely. Instead of working with difficult inpatients, I took a position in the hospital's outpatient clinic. There, I assessed and treated people living in the community, who, outwardly, were markedly less challenging than the psychotic people that had so fascinated me in my early professional years. It was a premeditated career change, as I decided to become proficient in long-term psychotherapy and one day enjoy a lucrative private practice.

In preparation for a career as a psychotherapist, I read abundantly on the theory and practice of psychotherapy and psychoanalysis. Unlike many colleagues, I did not regard psychoanalysis as the final word on human suffering and redemption but as a set of theoretical underpinnings of long-term, psychoanalytic therapies.

After one year at Topeka State Hospital, the wanderlust bug bit me yet again. Now I daydreamed of life in a big city, of live performances of symphonies by Beethoven and Shostakovich. My wife and I longed for furniture shops offering cool Scandinavian designs, rather than kitschy, American-made monstrosities. We considered resettling in San Francisco, New York, or Chicago—in that order. We thoroughly investigated, but the picture was bleak and discouraging, since those cities were riddled with crime and drugs. Public schools were egregious places for children to spend long hours in, and we would have to enrol our sons in private schools, so that they would receive a proper education. Alas, the combined salaries of a librarian and a psychologist would never be enough for private schools. Kerstin and I concluded, embittered, that our dream of living in an American metropolis might never materialize.

Here enters Lloyd, a Canadian-born, blond, blue-eyed, athletic-looking colleague. For reasons unknown to me, he had opted to earn not one but two master's degrees in psychology, instead of completing a doctoral-level education. Topeka State Hospital was a teaching hospital, and workers with MA degrees were assigned the rather tedious tasks of administering, scoring, and interpreting batteries of pencil-and-paper tests.

One day, as we reviewed Lloyd's reports, the clinic's secretary put through a long-distance call to me. It was the director of a clinic in Boston offering me the position of chief psychologist at his agency. We spoke for a minute or so, but the salary he offered was quite low, and I declined.

After hanging up, I turned to Lloyd, who was grinning at me provocatively.

"Looking for greener pastures?" he asked, ironic but sympathetic. "Oh, yes," I replied, slightly embarrassed because I had not informed my colleagues about my attempts to find a job in a major city. "You know how it is," I said more than a trifle apologetically. "People come to Topeka to get training. They stay in town for a few years, then move on."

"And where is your paradise located?" Lloyd teased.

I described the obstacles of settling down in an American metropolis.

"What about Toronto?" he challenged me.

"Why Toronto, of all places?" I asked, quite perplexed. I knew little about Canada, except that the "two solitudes" were a problem and that it boasted good health insurance programs.

"It's a big city with an opera and a ballet company," Lloyd went on, noticeably proud. "Some movie theatres show the European movies you like so much. As a matter of fact," he added, "I'm also looking for a job in Toronto. You have a PhD, Shalom, and you could get a good job just like that," he snapped his fingers.

I expressed reservations about the stratospherically high cost of private schools.

But Lloyd rhapsodized about Toronto's low crime rate, clean streets, and the multitudes of Italian and Portuguese immigrants infusing joie de vivre into the city. "As for public schools, they're crime-free and well maintained," he reassured me. "And there's a prominent Jewish community in Toronto. With a name like Shalom, it won't take long for you to become known to fellow Jews and start a select, profitable practice. Smarten up! You've been looking in the wrong places!"

That evening, Kerstin and I spoke at length about the implications of what Lloyd had told me. "So far," I summed up, "Toronto sounds like the right place for our family." The next few days we gathered information and decided to spend our annual vacation in the Toronto area.

That vacation was very pleasant. It was 1973, and in a pleasantly cool, cloudless summer day we got off the 401, the Windsor-to-Toronto highway, and drove up University Avenue. Like peasants marvelling at what a big city has to offer, we gazed in all directions. How clean and fresh and inspiring! We checked into a modest hotel and went for a walk, the first of many strolls.

After nine years of living in a small university town, Toronto struck me as a wealthy city, replete with luxury stores, a few great bookstores, and delightful eateries, a town much more appealing than Kansas City, Missouri, the Mecca for Kansans in search of big-city pleasures.

Of the many places we toured, one of the most impressive was the Kensington Market. In 1973 it featured many Portuguese stores and stalls, and I experienced it as a gripping déjà vu, as the short, stocky, moustachioed storekeepers reminded me of the Portuguese immigrants I had often encountered in my childhood in Rio de Janeiro. In a slight trance, I walked the streets of the market, marvelling at the signs in Portuguese, and taking in the sights and smells of what, in my eyes, looked like a Lusitanian village. I came across a few oval signs with Hebrew characters indicating that in the past some of the stores had featured kosher food.

During that vacation, my wife and I decided to make Toronto our home. Upon our return to Kansas, I set out to find a job in Toronto. Kerstin hoped to find a librarian's position once we were settled there. My recent appointment as group psychotherapy supervisor at the Menninger School of Psychiatry, an institution then offering some of the best training programs in psychiatry and psychology, opened quite a few doors. I learned there were a dozen graduates of the Menninger in Toronto, who proudly called themselves "The Menninger Mafia." One of them informed me of an opening in the psychology department at Toronto's Mount Sinai Hospital. I briefly corresponded with Bill, the chief of psychology, who invited me to a job interview.

In retrospect, my applying for a job as staff psychologist—and my character—was fraught with controversy. One senior psychiatrist who had interviewed me told Bill that hiring me would be like blurting out "Fuck you!" to his face. Apparently, that psychiatrist detested my immodest assertiveness and strongly opposed having me on board. The issue became a power struggle as Bill asserted his independence from psychiatry, while a few psychiatrists insisted on maintaining their traditional position of power and leadership. Things got so heated that I had to travel to Toronto for a second round of interviews. I was cognizant of the controversy I had involuntarily created but regarded it as a struggle between control freaks enmeshed in outmoded notions. I told myself that having a job in Toronto would be a foot in the door, and if things were not to my liking I would find another position. In 1974, jobs for psychologists were much easier to find than five years later. Before long, a letter notified me that I had a job waiting for me.

We arrived in Toronto in June 1974. It was very cold in the little house we'd rented, because the landlord had shut off the heat once the summer had officially arrived. Torontonians consoled us by recalling how, in early June just a few years before, it had been unseasonably chilly, and snow had whitened the streets and sidewalks.

Mount Sinai Hospital had recently moved to a new location, which Toronto wags called "The Sinai Hilton"—a luxurious-looking but essentially sterile building. The department of psychiatry was located on the ninth floor, divided into in- and outpatient areas. I met Bill and soon realized that, behind the façade of luxury, the entire ninth floor was a shambles: though Bill had fought tooth and nail to hire me, there was no available office awaiting me. Unlike my days of woe in Israel, I was full of beans and immediately set out to solve the problem of being "office-less."

It came to my attention, though, that there was in the outpatient clinic a huge, mostly unused, group therapy room. As I'd been hired to lead groups in a day treatment centre that never got off the ground while I worked at the hospital, Bill agreed to designate the group therapy room as my office.

From the hospital's warehouse I appropriated an enormous oak desk, a bright yellow swivelling chair, a dark-blue, three-seat sofa, a low coffee table, and a few upholstered chairs. The hospital administration agreed to install curtains to conceal the one-way mirror when there were no trainees observing group therapy sessions. My amused colleagues noted how quickly I had morphed from piteous schlemiel to group therapist working out of a humongous office equipped with state-of-the-art cameras and video-recording equipment.

Once installed in my office, I realized that the entire ninth floor was a pretentious, self-important, and quite deceitful place. In the inpatient ward, for instance, borderline patients—some of the most difficult-to-treat people—were scandalously hospitalized for months in order to undergo intensive psychotherapy with inexperienced residents in psychiatry. The sham was compounded by the novices being supervised by septuagenarian psychoanalysts in private practice with little experience in modern inpatient treatment.

There was, however, a great deal of staid, profound talk about treating "difficult patients"—a euphemism for what is commonly referred to as "borderline personality disorder." There was an unstated core belief that a novel label for ages-old issues would, as if by magic, accelerate the discovery of hitherto uncharted continents.

Psychiatrists, psychologists, and social workers staffed the outpatient clinic, of which I was a member. Not one of them ever challenged David Pinsker, the perpetually morose chief of psychiatry, who ran his fiefdom with a gloved iron fist. I survived the stifling ambience of slavish adherence to psychoanalytic theories and practices by poking fun at the establishment. One of my first quips was to refer to the entire ninth floor as "The Heights of Mount Sinai"—where God in the flesh, and not the archangel Gabriel, would every forty days reveal everlasting truths to the psychiatrists on staff, but to no one else.

To amuse myself, I invariably referred to one very orthodox and long-winded analyst as "What's-his-name?" Once, as a woman resident presented a paper on feminism and senescence, What's-his-name?—as if to vindicate me—embarked on a lengthy soliloquy on "the structure of neurosis." That notion might have been an original contribution before the First World War, but expatiating on it in 1975 struck me as a parody of What's-his-name? himself, and whatever he represented. I didn't, however, chortle, because a wave of sadness unexpectedly came over me: What's-his-name? now struck me as an old man doddering toward dementia, an elder in need of compassion, not jokes, barbs, and zingers.

In retrospect, I think I got away with buffoonery because of my good command of psychoanalytic theories, though I believed in only a fraction of what I had read. *Scientia potentia est*, knowledge is power, especially when you're dealing with speculations no empirical research can ever disprove. My combativeness regarding prevalent theories was, to a large extent, an outgrowth of my Jewish education. Consciously, I was putting into practice the Mishnaic saying attributed to Rabbi Elazar: "Know what to reply to Epicureans!" The Epicureans' hedonism was anathema to the rabbis, but in contemporary terms one could say, "Be well-informed! Study your opponents and knowledgeably debate them!"

As for my work, I believe I proved my mettle whenever discussions of clinical practices arose, as I voiced opinions without advertising, pseudo-modestly, my empathic understanding of my patients. My therapy groups, for instance, were regularly observed by medical students, interns, and residents in psychiatry, and my skills—and failings—were at all times on display. My colleagues, on the other hand, interminably debated the evil and occasional wonders of countertransference—the impact of a therapist's unresolved neuroses on the treatment he is conducting. And yet they would never allow anyone to observe them in action. Their countertransference took place behind hermetically closed doors.

I don't believe I am stupid. I was well aware that behind my back I was referred to as "narcissist"—a perception I did absolutely nothing to dispel, and at times went out of my way to reinforce, since it inspired me and enhanced my creativity. I basked in an aura of irreverence for authority and mockery of my supposed betters. (Already then, I had noticed that people in general, and therapists in particular, would call you a "narcissist" if they detested you. But if they hated you with a passion, and wished you were slowly, ever so slowly, tortured to death, they would call you a "psychopath.")

A great taboo, one rarely mentioned let alone elaborated on, is the overrepresentation of Jews in psychoanalytic circles. Early in the twentieth century, for example, Freud's followers in Vienna were a group of Jewish doctors, except for Carl Gustav Jung, their token goy. Later, when New York became the Mecca of psychoanalysis, Jews continued to be highly overrepresented, a fact neither discussed nor joked about. In Toronto, we Jews are a relatively small community, and yet the percentage of Jews among analysts is exceedingly high—a stark reality swept under the rug not only by the converted but by critics too. The latter hold their tongues for fear of being branded racist or anti-Semitic.

My attitude toward psychoanalysis is ambivalent, no doubt. I admire some aspects of it, but I dislike much of what I have read and heard. I myself, a Brazilian-born whose first language is Portuguese, feel understood when I recall Vinicius de Moraes, a Brazilian poet, songwriter, playwright, diplomat, and journalist. Once, while being interviewed, he was asked, "Given Brazil's political, economic, and cultural circumstances, what do you think would be most beneficial: capitalism or socialism?"

Unhesitating, Vinicius cried out, "Socialism, *but with samba*!"

Now "samba" meant not only exuberant rhythms and melodies, or costumed, almost-naked women and men singing and dancing and frolicking. It also implied that nothing should be taken completely seriously, since no one is above scathing witticisms, ironies, and jokes. Though beautiful, great samba contains a great deal of melancholy and wistful yearnings—*saudades*—such as the realization that Carnival lasts five days in February, not a lifetime.

In my eyes, psychotherapy-but-with-samba meant that a therapist at work is frequently intuitive, spontaneous, humorous, and ironic rather than intellectual, analytical, and speculative. As Goethe wondrously put it, "All theory is grey, but green is the golden tree of life." Psychotherapy, like samba, is essentially tragic, as we all accomplish only a fraction of our dreams and reveries.

Years later, over lunch, I discussed psychotherapy-but-with-samba with Howard Bacal, a training analyst—an analysts' analyst—who, like me, was much interested in group therapy. He did occasionally ask me to assess some of his patients, and I felt he valued my findings and recommendations. He listened as I elaborated on my version of psychotherapy, he asked me a couple of questions, and yet I sensed he was annoyed with my unorthodox, irreverent notions. A while later, I regretted sharing my views with Howard, as months before I had been hospitalized for runaway mania, and he probably regarded my views as a recovering madman's preoccupations.

I continued practising as I saw fit but mentioned my but-with-samba approach infrequently, as my colleagues conducted their work in a grave and solemn manner, and lampooning the competition was the only form of humour they approved of. Psychoanalysts, for instance, mocked cognitive behaviour therapists over their alleged superficiality; the latter, in turn, spared no bile while describing the mediocre results of traditional psychotherapy.

Throughout, I advised my patients that I practised "insight-oriented psychotherapy" and applied whatever insights I deemed helpful for a given patient. I would, for instance, mention ideas borrowed from psychoanalysis, cognitive therapy, or evolutionary psychology. I periodically queried my patients whether or not I was making sense, to ensure that my interpretations were not confusing or unnecessarily distressing them.

After moving to Toronto, my wife and I yearned to buy a house, and to make that goal possible I began to see private patients on hospital premises, even during working hours. This was technically not permitted, but all of my colleagues supplemented their income with a private practice on the side. Truth be told, none of us saw many hospital patients, as we saved our energies and dedication for our well-paying private charges. I soothed my guilty conscience by claiming, quite disingenuously, that while in Rome I behaved as Romans did. I swept that hunk of amorality under the carpet by persuading myself that I needed a home for my family and was in dire need of cash.

From 1974 to 1977, I was overflowing with energy and enthusiasm—what would eventually morph into violent mania. I must emphasize that though I was continually excited and enthusiastic, I was neither psychotic nor hypomanic at that time. Only decades later did Dr. Sagar Parikh, an expert on bipolar disorder, assuage my dread of becoming sick by reassuring me that there is such a thing as "a normal high," like the moments when I was pleased with my clinical work or my writing.

Though very taxing, I enjoyed working with schizophrenic people in groups and was often very involved in that line of work. Once, when Janice, a member of one of my groups, did not show up for a session, I asked those in attendance what was the matter with her. It turned out that Janice was thinking of overdosing on the dozens of antidepressants she'd for months been stashing away. I chose to intervene by tapping and tapping my wristwatch with a forefinger while declaring, "I expect you guys to have Janice right here, in this room, in twenty minutes! I've no idea how you guys are going to pull that off. All I know for certain is that you *will* do it!"

In half an hour Janice was in my office, meekly apologizing for the tumult she had unwittingly created. With an hour left in the session, I chose to explore, in detail, each member's reaction to my conduct in the group, to Janice's suicidal plans, and whether they too had recently considered killing themselves. Following that session, the group's cohesion and participation in the discussions improved a great deal.

All told, my clinical work brought me great satisfaction. Fifteen years later, when I began, at long last, to write fiction, I encouraged myself with, "I'll be happy the day the stories I write are as good as the psychotherapy I daily perform."

WHAT CHANGED THE COURSE OF MY ILLNESS, AND THE directions my life took, was my acquaintance with Ruth Easser, a psychoanalyst who consulted at my hospital. She had been a renowned analyst in New York and, for reasons unknown to me, she and her husband, also a training analyst, had moved to Toronto. A tall and lanky woman, she had a pleasant-looking, long face framing forever-alert brown eyes and a thin nose. Bill, the chief of psychology, made arrangements for Ruth to supervise his staff weekly.

In one meeting, I presented the case of a single woman with numerous problems at work and recurring conflicts with her mother and rebellious son. Weekly she would bombard me with inane details about her work, and avoided discussions of the personal issues that had driven her to seek therapy. I discussed at some length my frustration at the impasse I was experiencing. Without chiding me, Ruth softly commented that my frustration must have come across to my patient. "How can anyone hide it completely?" she challenged not only me but questioningly eyed each one of my colleagues. Then she added that I was not being empathetic: "Your role," she said, "is to be with that woman where she's at, what she thinks is important. Therapy sessions are her time with you, and she can use it any way she sees fit!" Ruth's oracular pronouncements made me blush because her comments rang true. Indeed, I had been an impatient clod, and had not been sufficiently compassionate and attentive.

During the next several sessions with that woman, I paid close attention to her complaints, even sided with her over the menial nature of her work. Soon she exhausted all of her complaints about her job, and on her own began exploring family problems at great length. My admiration of Ruth Easser's directness and helpfulness knew no bounds. I had witnessed her acumen, sensitivity, and capacity for empathy. Though she had pointed out my faults, she did it without embarrassing me. I was entirely taken by her capacity to assess quickly the ongoing therapies presented to her without mentioning facile, intellectualized notions like countertransference or Oedipal conflicts. I attended her group supervision with a great deal of enthusiasm.

Through the grapevine I found out that she could be quite confrontational too. One resident in psychiatry told me, more amused than angry, how Ruth had commented that his therapy with a borderline woman was going nowhere. He was told he was allowing his patient "to crap right between your eyes" without reacting, as if he were watching a show on TV. The resident and I laughed with abandon at Ruth's intervention, and delighted in her helpful directness. Other staff spoke of her kindness, while still others praised her spontaneity and artlessness.

The more I worked with Ruth, the more I appreciated her version of psychoanalysis. One day, on utter impulse, I decided to be analyzed by her, not because I believed in the theories she espoused but because of her—her style, honesty, clear thinking and emphasis on obtaining results. That would have complemented my treatment in Israel, and I would, once and for all, deal with my capitulation to helplessness and despair.

I called Ruth's private office and requested an appointment. The financial aspects of psychoanalysis were not a problem: the cost of therapy with psychiatrists in Ontario was fully and limitlessly covered by the provincial health insurance plan. "What the hell," I reasoned, "why not be analyzed when the taxpayers of Ontario will foot 90 percent of the bill?"

Dr. Easser's office was located not far from what some called "Angst Alley"—the row of houses along St. Clair Avenue where many psychotherapists had their offices. I took the elevator to her suite and encountered a spacious waiting room. As with all my appointments, I'd come ten minutes early. Heart pounding and fingers gently tingling,

I read some of the waiting room's magazines to calm myself down.

She was a few minutes late, wearing a white, satiny, long-sleeved blouse and tweedy, salt-and-pepper pants. We shook hands, and I took notice of her tired-looking eyes. What, I asked myself, is she exhausted at eleven o'clock already? During supervision at the hospital, I'd seen her as alert as a sleuth searching for clues leading to a conviction. A sleepy analyst is not what I need, I thought.

She showed me into her spacious office, which sported a large curtained window. An air conditioner whirred monotonously. I sat on the edge of a brown corduroy wing chair, whereas she perched on a black Eames chair. "How can I help you, Shalom?" she asked, peering into my eyes.

I was surprised. I'd expected her to be nondirective and wait for me to carry the ball. Her straightforward question spoiled the speech I had prepared and rehearsed for the occasion. "Well, I would like..." I said haltingly, "to start my analysis...with you...I don't believe in a lot of psychoanalytic theories...but...I'm interested. I would like you...to be my analyst. I like your approach...I like...*you*!" I paused to examine her tired face.

She smiled feebly, seemingly amused by a callow applicant such as myself. "To be successfully analyzed," she forcefully said, "you don't have to believe in any theories! Psychoanalysis is not a *cult*! All I expect my patients to do is to come on time, lie on the couch, try hard to free associate, and pay attention to what I'm saying." She briefly smiled, and I felt embarrassed for having talked like a fool. Before I managed to respond, she added, "At any rate, I cannot be your analyst. Haven't you heard about my illness?"

"No," I said, stunned.

"I have advanced lung cancer." She paused, and I felt unforgivably ashamed of bothering a dying woman with my petty concerns. "I'm very sorry to hear about that," I mumbled.

"The treatment is worse than the disease! Chemotherapy is terribly fatiguing." For a moment she seemed buried in thought. "But I'm so glad I was analyzed," she said animatedly. "I was then ten years younger than you're now, and it really helps me to cope with my imminent death." For quite a while she looked askance, then, remembering the purpose of our meeting, she said firmly, "There's no shortage of good analysts in Toronto." She recommended a man and a woman unknown to me. By now I felt our meeting had become surreal: I was talking to a dying person about my plans for the next few years, while her days were numbered. It shocked me to realize I was saying *adieu* to her, not *au revoir*, since she would no longer be consulting at the hospital, I assumed. She stood up and extended her hand. "I would have loved to talk about your analysis, but I must save my energies for the few patients I'm still seeing. Good luck!" She sounded as direct and spontaneous as always. I thanked her effusively for seeing me at her office and shook her dry, bony, and cold hand. I was, indeed, shaking hands with a woman about to die.

She died two weeks later, and I was shaken by the loss. Months later, I heard that a psychiatrist in analysis with Ruth had been so traumatized by her dying that for six months he was incapable of doing any work. At length I spoke with my colleagues about Ruth's death and my disappointment with not having her as my analyst. One psychiatrist I liked told me that Stan Lesser, Ruth's husband, was her training analyst, and she was very pleased with his unorthodox, empathetic stance. Two weeks after his wife's funeral I called him, and he offered me an appointment.

Stan Lesser's office was in the same condo as his deceased wife's. Seated in an upholstered chair in their waiting room, I thought of how they'd been life partners and colleagues working side by side. I recalled a classic article on "hysteroid" personalities they had co-authored, Ruth's name appearing first. I had no idea whether the latter was due to alphabetical reasons, or that she had been the article's lead author.

In a few minutes I shook hands with an unsmiling, pasty-faced Doctor Lesser. He was a tall, bulky man who carried his weight well. His fat lower lip protruded, and his dark brown eyes conveyed determination. He smelled of coffee and cigarette smoke, but nothing in his face or bearing suggested grief over his deceased wife.

He led me to his office, and we climbed some stairs side by side. That surprised me, as I'd heard of analysts walking steps ahead of their patients, leaving them to fend for themselves, so as to assess their capacity to behave autonomously.

Like his late wife, Stan didn't strike me as rigid or uptight. His office was long and narrow, probably a bedroom before the condo's conversion to offices. Along one wall sat the obligatory brown leather couch.

As we sat down, he lit a cigarette but didn't offer me one. I was, however, too excited, too nervous to light one of my own. He asked me how he could help me, and I told him of my attachment to his late wife. I elaborated on my wish to enter analysis with her, despite my criticisms of psychoanalytic theories and practices.

He placed his cigarette on the ashtray on his desk. "You know I'm a training analyst, don't you?" His voice was gravelly and a bit hard to follow. "Most people seeing me want to become analysts one day. Have you considered that?"

"Only after meeting Doctor Easser in person did I decide to have an analysis," I said.

"Good," he said. "I've heard about your work with schizophrenics. It would be worthwhile if one day you did psychoanalytic group therapy with outpatients and wrote it up."

I felt flattered. His alluding to my work augured well.

"Tell me about your life these days."

In some detail, I told him about my wife having vaginal bleedings and her many fears and worries.

"Is she ill?" he fired.

"That's the problem! Her condition hasn't been diagnosed, the treatment is unclear, and she fears she's about to die. I think she's very anxious because that's a very delicate matter."

"Are you concerned that she might die?"

To me, that question sounded inappropriate, probably rooted in his own grief. I remembered my wife's numerous, emotionally draining complaints about her bleedings, and my back went up. Tell him like it is, I told myself, then turned to him. "I think hers is a relatively minor problem. But if she is seriously ill and about to die, I hope she will, for her own sake, die with dignity."

He winced, my comment probably stinging him. I felt we had come closer to one another, as he had just lost his wife to cancer, while I was struggling with my wife's dread of illness and of death. He fell silent, and I elaborated on how my wife's complaints made me apprehensive, despite my determination not to succumb to her pessimism.

He said nothing, and I felt that my bringing up death with dignity had somehow affected him personally. His wife, I had heard, had acted in a dignified manner to the very end. Was I too blunt, too direct with someone grieving a life partner? I asked myself. As he kept silent, I spoke about how I disliked my work at the hospital. I mentioned briefly my severe upset in Israel, and I praised Dr. Tamarin's unorthodox, but helpful, treatment. He asked whether I had felt depressed recently, and I emphasized my good health. At the end of the interview he said I could start my analysis next week.

"Usually," he said gravely, "I see people in a training analysis four times a week. If you decide not to get into training, we'll cut down to three sessions a week."

"I'll be seeing you four times a week," I replied, carried away by impulsivity. While talking with Dr. Lesser, I decided to give psychoanalytic training a try, in part because I sensed that was what both the late Ruth and he expected of me. Looking back on that initial interview, it is clear that I wasn't assessed properly, as he didn't inquire how disabling or incapacitating my depression in Israel had been, and he asked no questions about whether or not I had had suicidal thoughts. Dr. Tamarin's erroneous diagnosis of my disturbance was a forgivable mistake. My analyst, on the other hand, didn't ask me very crucial questions, and my family and I ended up paying exorbitantly for those omissions.

A week after my initial interview, I was back on Dr. Lesser's couch. I remembered my futile clashes with Dr. Tamarin over whether or not to lie on a couch, and I decided not to repeat that inconsequential experience. He sat on a leather chair right behind my head and lit a cigarette. I started by discussing my wife's bleedings. That was a bad start: I lay on a couch without my personal history being examined in depth. I rationalized Dr. Lesser's flaw by telling myself that was his style and that he would get to know my background as the analysis progressed. But in all the time I was in therapy with him we never discussed my disastrous meltdown in Israel.

The issue of whether or not to embark on formal training in psychoanalysis was resolved rather quickly. I had two interviews with training analysts and expressed my honest feelings that psychoanalysis might be a prestigious club and yet I felt ambivalent about both theory and practices. Prior to my third interview, the Lakeshore Psychiatric Hospital, which I had been consulting with, informed me that they were cutting down on staff and my position would be terminated in two weeks. That announcement infuriated me, and in my interview with a third analyst I angrily vociferated my sense of humiliation. With tears in my eyes, I stated that I couldn't possibly afford the lengthy, expensive supervision required of neophyte analysts. Days later, a letter from the Toronto Psychoanalytic Institute notified me that my application for training had been rejected. I felt relieved, as others had cut the Gordian knot and dissolved my ambivalence. I felt good telling Dr. Lesser I would be seeing him three times a week.

The first months of my analysis were dull and boring. Unlike my therapy with Dr. Tamarin, I had no crippling symptoms to complain about. I remember chatting about my work, my colleagues, my wife, and my children—nothing that set the world on fire. Dr. Lesser smoked almost incessantly, he responded quite often, but mumbled a great deal. "This can't go on," I admonished myself, and the next day I pulled a cigarette out of a package of mine, lit it, and puffed at it with gusto.

He harrumphed, then exclaimed, "You know you're not supposed to gratify impulses during your analysis!"

I laughed, pleased with myself. "Look who's calling the kettle black!"

He went silent, but I continued, "You forgot to mumble and now you choose to stay quiet. Why don't we discuss how come *you* smoke during my sessions? What about you gratifying your impulses?"

He kept mum, and I chain-smoked till the end of that session. The next session I lit a cigarette right after I lay down, and he said I was defying his authority. This time I said nothing. Our chats about my relationship with colleagues went on for a few weeks, and I was growing increasingly bored and wondered what I could do to start enjoying my analysis.

One day, I sat up on the couch and told a surprised Dr. Lesser a story: how Albert Einstein spent half an hour a week with a blond girl of about eight. His assistants were flabbergasted, as they couldn't understand these goings-on, what with great physicists the world over waiting for months before Einstein would spend fifteen minutes with them. Finally, one of Einstein's assistants asked the great man what he was doing with the little girl every week.

"Oh," smiled Einstein, "I teach her arithmetic. She's not very good at it, and it takes time before she gets it."

"But professor," exclaimed one indignant assistant, "I'll be glad to teach the girl so that you could confer with two more theoretical physicists each week."

"Oh no!" Einstein objected. "You wouldn't believe what *amazing* cookies she brings me every week."

Dr. Lesser laughed a lot, then asked me, "Did you make up that story?"

"I'm not sure if I made it up, doc, or read it somewhere. When I'm in a good mood, I believe I concocted it."

"What's the purpose of telling me that story?" Dr. Lesser asked as he lit another cigarette.

"It has a lot to do with my analysis, doc," I mirthfully replied. "For months I've been chatting away, trying to impress you. Einstein's assistants also second-guessed what would please the great physicist. It turned out he was more interested in tasty cookies than in meeting colleagues. So I've decided to be myself and stop trying to impress you!"

He flung his hand. "So why don't you lie on the couch and get down to it?"

I slowly stretched out on the couch. I was silent for a long while, then said, "I don't believe I've told you about Isa, the black Brazilian woman who raised me from age ten months until I turned six. She, and not my mother, was the most important figure in my early life. That's one reason I don't believe in any theories about mothering, overprotective mothers, good-enough mothers, clinical mothers, schizophrenogenic mothers, refrigerator mothers—and what have you." After briefly pausing, I said, "Psychoanalysts keep constructing a palatial edifice in which they house mothers and mothering. They confine me, a dyed-in-the-wool individualist, to the windowless, wet, and smelly basement of their building!"

During the following sessions I elaborated on my love for Isa, but my analyst remained silent throughout my revelations. He asked no inspiring questions and I believe he didn't understand that my passion for Isa far surpassed any and all of my feelings for my tepid mother. Luckily, Harry Hardin, a training analyst and good friend of mine, was doing research on patients brought up by someone other than their biological mothers, like nannies, grandparents, or aunts. He helped me a lot by explaining how the culturally biased emphasis on the merits of biological mothers often eclipses the unresolved feelings some people harbour over the loss of those figures that had actually mothered them. "Dr. Lesser failed to understand how the loss of a beloved woman, who had for years mothered you, was a traumatic event," Harry told me.

After a series of conversations with Harry, I realized that, many decades after Isa had left me, I still mourned her abandoning me. And years later, the first work of fiction I ever completed depicted the mad love of a Jewish little boy for his black Brazilian nanny of sorts. It took me five years of laborious rewriting and editing until I felt that my novella captured the boy's love for that woman and his dread that she would one day abandon him. My self-discoveries led to growing restlessness at work and at home; I was becoming increasingly agitated, but neither my analyst nor I suspected that arrant madness was faintly knocking on my door.

A major precipitant of my first manic episode was a research project that enthused me immensely. I was trying to answer a fundamental question: What is the human condition of schizophrenic people when they are not outright psychotic? Ever since Eugen Bleuler first described the "group of schizophrenias," clinicians' attention has focussed on these people's psychoses, such as their hallucinations, delusions, thought disorders, and paranoia. But how did schizophrenics experience themselves and the world when they were not indisputably mad?

These questions arose out of my treatment of schizophrenics in groups, when group members quite often were not overtly psychotic, either because of the medication they were taking or because some patients were moderately disturbed. After exhaustive research on my patients' clinical records, I came to the conclusion that three features characterized nonpsychotic schizophrenic people's lives: dis-ease, dis-order, and despair. They rarely felt at ease in a world peopled by humans and containing innumerable man-made objects and institutions. While mad, I learned, those people practically never experienced delusions about naturally occurring things like mountains, rivers, snow, or rain. Rather, they dreaded people or human products, such as medications, hospitals, or the FBI. Their experiences, I claimed, were fluid and lacked coherence or a sense of wholeness.

I convinced myself that I had discovered an uncharted continent: namely, schizophrenics lived in despair of being mired in dis-eased and dis-ordered lives. They had limited incentive to live. My ideas, I knew, were quite convoluted and difficult to grasp by colleagues trained to think of schizophrenia as an aggregate of psychotic symptoms.

Since I worked in isolation from colleagues, I had found no suitable forum to present my views. After several inquiries, I called Dr. Vivian Rakoff, a professor of psychiatry known for erudition and tolerance of new ideas. We met in his office, where countless books crowded the shelves, and others were piled up high on the floor. He was a short man of about fifty-five, his eyes black-brown and penetrating, a man thirsty for novelty and information. We briefly spoke about our views on family therapy, a treatment of interest to both of us. Finally, he sat up in his swivelling chair and asked, "How can I help you?"

I discussed at some length the issue of schizophrenic people being nonpsychotic some of the time, which piqued his curiosity. His hand motioned me to go on, so I explained my research on the three *D*s of schizophrenia and how delusions revolved on man-made objects and institutions, never about mountains or clouds.

For a long while he looked askance, as if searching for ways to confute my theories. Suddenly, he faced me again and said that I ought to write an article about my views for the *Review of Existential Psychiatry and Psychology*. Feeling a bit recognized, a wave of pride washed over me. I thanked him for his support, and he amiably agreed to read a draft of my article.

Next day, before dawn, I began writing lengthy notes in preparation for writing the book I felt destined to bring into the world. My moods, however, soared furiously, and instead of writing an article, I ceaselessly daydreamed about an epochal opus, *The Human Condition of Schizophrenic People*. In the magisterial tome I daydreamed of, I would expound on my ideas and become a thinker as eminent as Karl Jaspers, a psychiatrist and influential existentialist philosopher I admired. As I grew increasingly grandiose, I slept less and less, and nightly worked on my book, from nine in the evening till two in the morning, or even later. My sleep disorder worsened by the day, and I began drinking vodka at bedtime, as it was difficult for me to fall asleep.

I shared my sleeplessness with my analyst, but he didn't react with alarm, as he should have, probably thinking I was in the throes of a "creative neurosis," or some other mid-seventies buzzword. At the time, it surprised me that I didn't feel at all tired during the day, despite my unremitting sleeplessness. Rather, I felt energetic and enthusiastic, and could hardly wait for the evening to come so I could work on my book.

I must point out that my attempt to write a book never progressed beyond making copious notes. As a manic episode soon took over my life, instead of writing on schizophrenia I had to confront my own psychosis. My cherished notions of the three *D*s said to characterize schizophrenic people were not, however, entirely lost or abandoned. Years later, I wrote *Nine Ninety-Nine*, a novel about a paranoid schizophrenic writer. In the novel, the entirely mad narrator relates how his love poem, "The Meaning of Madness," depicted insanity along the lines of the three *D*s I had so ecstatically conceived.

Chapter 4

First Ascent into Madness

IN FEBRUARY 1977, I FLEW TO SAN FRANCISCO TO attend the annual convention of the American Group Psychotherapy Association. I was scheduled to present a paper on my work with schizophrenic people in a symposium on group therapy for people with psychotic illnesses.

Prior to presenting my paper, I participated in an Institute—an experiential event where therapists become members of a group interacting for two days. The Institute I attended was led by a confrontational leader, who repeatedly put members on the "hot seat" over their supposed symptoms and conflicts. To me it felt like therapy rather than a learning experience, and I became so incensed that I vociferously complained to the convention's organizers. In retrospect, I was already then highly aroused and dangerously excitable after two days of group discussions. I barely slept the night before I presented my paper.

Nonetheless, the symposium went very well; I read my paper with a great deal of enthusiasm. I answered questions from the audience in detail and humorously. A white-haired, grandfatherly looking man stood up and remarked, "Shalom is an evocative-provocative group leader." I felt flattered by his complimentary observation.

A severe bout of insomnia came over me that night, and I tossed and turned in bed, as I mulled over being called "evocative-provocative." I slept very little and waited almost four hours for a daylong experiential workshop I'd signed up for, as its leader was a renowned clinician from Los Angeles whose last name was King. To kill time, I read and reread passages from a Bible I found in the bedside table. Despite my growing giddiness, I became absorbed in the scriptural tales of parents favouring one child over other siblings. In my growing confusion, those stories seemed immensely relevant to me, personally.

The workshop ran all day, with a break for lunch. I remember being very talkative throughout the workshop, and I repeatedly interrupted others until the workshop leader asked me to let others participate. Attending that workshop was a psychiatrist from Barrie, Ontario, who told me, months later, that I seemed extremely excited at the workshop and repeatedly quoted the Bible. "All of it was very bizarre," that colleague said, "because whatever you said somehow reflected the goings-on throughout the workshop."

Next morning I was in a daze as a cab drove me to the airport. While on route to Chicago, where I was to change planes, I was in a panic and frantically summoned the flight attendant. She soon appeared, and I had a vision: the flight attendant's face was aglow while the entire cabin behind her looked utterly black. I was so agitated I could barely speak. The attendant asked the passenger next to me to stand up, and she sat next to me, patting my forearm as she talked. My guardian angel vetted my boarding pass and said, "Everything will be all right. I'll help you change planes in Chicago, and you'll return to Toronto safely."

I basked in her numinous, shining face, but my heart was pounding. About to faint, I groped for her hand and clutched it. "What's your name?" I asked, and she kindly said, "I'm Gloria Vincent." I vowed I'd write the president of American Airlines about the wonderful help she gave me.

I have no memories of changing planes, or flying to Toronto. What I do remember is getting out of a cab idling right in front of our townhouse and climbing up the stairs to the door. Months after I'd partially recovered, Kerstin told me that I had acted very strangely, as I didn't hug and kiss her or our children, and looked dazed. Our children looked disappointed, since they'd drawn colourful pictures to celebrate my coming home, and there I was, ignoring them.

My wife tried in vain to engage me in a rational conversation, but all I would talk about was Gloria Vincent's radiant beauty. Kerstin urged me to call Dr. Lesser and tell him what was happening. It was Sunday afternoon, and, luckily, I got in touch with him.

"Dr. Lesser," I bugled, "it's Shalom calling. I feel tired, but basically I'm just fine. My wife wanted me to call you."

"It's the first time you've called me," he replied gruffly. "What's going on?"

"I got excited, on the plane. It was dark, and I summoned the flight attendant. She was, she is, a ravishing beauty, and her face glowed like a full moon. Her name is Gloria, and she—"

"Where are you now?" He sounded more angry than alarmed, and I wondered what I had done wrong.

"At home," I said.

"Is your wife with you?"

"Yes."

"Good. I'll be seeing you tomorrow at ten, your regular time."

"Sure. But I really must tell you how beautiful Gloria is—"

"Did something happen in San Francisco?"

"I was told I'm an evocative-provocative therapist. I read the Bible and talked about it in the workshop chaired by the king of Los Angeles and—"

"You're *hypomanic*!" he exclaimed. "I'll be calling your pharmacy to prescribe Valium. Take two pills now and two more at bedtime. I'll see you tomorrow morning. Take care."

Months later, I learned that prescribing Valium to a person in my condition was bad therapy, as the Valium did almost nothing to calm me down, and I raved and ranted endlessly. By then, Kerstin had tears streaming down her cheeks, and I finally shut up and distractedly watched a football game on TV.

I slept about two hours that night, and woke up while it was still dark outside. I could neither lie still in bed nor read a book. I began to walk up and down the staircase, finally settling down to watch a TV show I couldn't concentrate on. When Kerstin awoke, she asked what I would do that morning.

"Go to work!" I yelled. "You're meddling with my life and that bugs the hell out of me!"

"But Shalom," she implored, "you can't go to the hospital in your condition."

"I've got to be there! I have patients waiting. You're a librarian, and your books can always wait. But my patients need me, and I must be there for them!"

"Call the hospital," she held my hand, "tell them you're ill. You can't show up for work when you're not well."

"You always worry about what others think. I'm going!" I shouted, and she gestured that I was upsetting the kids. "You hear me?" I hollered. "Nobody can stop me!"

That morning I had no patients scheduled until noon. I sat in my office and endeavoured to read the *Schizophrenia Bulletin*, but soon realized that my mind was roving in all directions. I had a cup of coffee in the hospital cafeteria, and when I came back there was a message from my analyst, asking me to call him at 10:55, just before his eleven o'clock patient. I called, and he emphatically asked, "How are you?"

"I'm fine. I'm in my office, trying to read."

"You didn't show up for your ten o'clock appointment," he said warmly, as if to compensate for his brusqueness the day before. "I must see you at twelve fifteen."

"I'll see you at twelve fifteen," I said, immensely disturbed because I'd badly goofed by forgetting my ten o'clock appointment. "What else am I doing wrong," I wondered.

An unsmiling, visibly tense Dr. Lesser met me in the waiting room. Undaunted, I went straight to the couch, lay down, and went on to tell him about San Francisco and my flight home. He was more active than usual, asking questions whenever I stopped talking. It was, once again, lousy therapy to try to continue psychoanalysis when I had been hypomanic the day before. He should have insisted on me sitting up and us having a no-nonsense talk about my serious condition. A competent psychiatrist would have right away prescribed an antipsychotic and a mood stabilizer, such as lithium.

I calmed down slightly over the next few days, but hypomania soon returned. I barely slept because of my overexcitement, my speech fast and pressured. I became furious at home because my teary wife yet again begged me not to show up at the hospital. "You're unwell," she insisted, but in a rage I accused her of driving me crazy.

At the hospital, I began pestering my co-workers with incessant patter, jokes, and patting them on the back, suddenly buddy-buddy with all of humankind. After working hours, I went on shopping sprees, buying Bibles in every language I'd ever studied, Latin and Arabic included. I began to obsess about the meanings lurking behind book titles, since they somehow contributed to the research I was doing.

It became hard for me to sit down for more than a few minutes, and while not at home or at work I prowled the streets, going from bookstore to bookstore, buying books in history and philosophy. In retrospect, I was preparing myself for a scholarly career, though it would have flabbergasted me had anyone suggested that.

My work suffered. I became too humorous with patients, too often challenging or confronting them with issues I should have approached subtly, gradually, and cautiously. The few patients who were aware of my attending a convention commented that I must have learned new techniques that I was now experimenting with. In my therapy groups patients laughed too much and became garrulous and confrontational in response to my elation and restlessness. Meanwhile, I continued my analysis, reporting on my increasingly excitable behaviour. One Friday after work, I met with Harry Hardin, who had recently been appointed a training analyst. We sat in his office facing each other as he listened, looking intrigued, to my plans to visit Weimer, in then East Germany, as a way of immersing myself in

Goethe's poetry. I rambled about brushing up on the German I'd studied in graduate school, and then I handed him Part I and II of *Faust*, in German, that I'd just bought on the way to his office. Harry looked stern, his piercing eyes disconcerting me. "Are you seeing Dr. Lesser?" He leaned forward, and I glimpsed his bald crown.

"Yes, three times a week."

He sat back, as if rehearsing the punch line he was about to deliver. "And are you sitting up, or lying on the couch?"

"On the couch," I cried out proudly.

"I think you need to sit up and talk turkey!" I knew Harry as a straight shooter that regarded intellectualizing as the worst crime a psychoanalyst could commit. He had few followers, but those who admired him treasured his uncompromising frankness. I envied his humorous and good-natured style of challenging patients and friends, so that unpalatable insights turned into witty ironies that made people laugh. I paused to consider the implications of what I had just heard. Was I so disturbed that my analysis must come to an end?

In a moment, Harry cut the crap. "And what is Dr. Lesser doing about your *psychosis*?"

Psychosis? Outright madness? I shuddered, heart pounding my ribs. "Nothing," I eventually replied.

"You look agitated, slimmer than usual, and way too talkative. Have you lost weight?"

"Twelve pounds."

"And how are you sleeping?"

"Very poorly."

"And your concentration?"

"Really shitty."

Harry's eyes were now expressing alarm. "When are you seeing Dr. Lesser next?"

"Monday, at ten. Do you mind if I quote you on the psychosis bit?"

He patted my upper arm. "Be my guest!"

Over the weekend, I pondered my psychosis of sorts. It explained why my colleagues were keeping away from me, and my wife's unceasing worries. At that stage of my illness, no one but Harry, a superb judge of character, suspected that I was dangerously ill. Just as Dr. Tamarin had misdiagnosed me, Dr. Lesser and my co-workers had failed to grasp how truly unhinged I was, and not suffering from some minor ailment caused by an analysis gone wrong. I paid an exorbitant price for this error in judgment, and for many weeks I went without the medication I urgently needed. Those around me had been caught in the web of dogma, and failed to see I was becoming sicker and in need of *medical* treatment, and not some brainy mumbo-jumbo. I give Harry credit for being the first to recognize that I was not some "casualty" of psychoanalysis and group experiences.

Looking back, it's evident that the strain of my analysis, plus the stress of the convention, sparked off a manic condition, just as the stress of resettling in Israel had triggered a severe depression. Knowing what I know today, it is clear that I should never have entered psychoanalysis, which is appropriate only for those with good ego-strength—a strong psychological constitution, in plain English. I, it turned out, was more brittle than my therapists and I ever thought.

One Monday morning, when I saw my analyst, I told him I wouldn't be lying on the couch but would, instead, role-play the different components of my self. Before he uttered a word, I began to play the role of psychologist administering the Rorschach inkblot test. First I handed a card to an imaginary patient, and then I wrote down his responses verbatim. Looking perturbed, Dr. Lesser asked how I was feeling.

"Great!" I bellowed. "Now watch this!" I stood up and began to play the role of infantry soldier. I supposedly fired a machine gun from the hip, as I had done during basic training in Israel. Then I placed two outstretched fingers on my upper arm to convey that a year later I'd been promoted to corporal.

I was enjoying to the hilt my capacity to petrify my analyst. He looked very alarmed, in a panic even. Before he reacted, I showed off what had been drilled into me: I stood up, took a step forward, and bayonetted an enemy soldier. Then I fell back one short step and twisted my notional rifle counter-clockwise and winkled it out from the enemy's gut with a powerful kick to the groin. I felt ecstatic, a murderous rage holding sway over me.

"Sit down, Shalom," my panicking analyst begged me. "Take a deep breath!"

Dr. Lesser was breathing rapidly and his nostrils were flaring up, perhaps because he believed I might kill him. He pulled out a pack of cigarettes, fished one out, then put it to his lips. I violently motioned that I too wanted to smoke. He offered me his pack, and I wedged a cigarette between my lips, lit a match, then graciously offered him a light. I laughed at my phony, exaggerated politeness.

"I'd like to see you and your wife tomorrow, at nine o'clock," he said after exhaling deeply, an attempt to contain his dread.

I laughed loudly, then said, "She works. She can't come."

"Tell her it's urgent. In the meantime, I'll be making arrangements."

I felt as if my head was bathing in a warm, thick fluid. I didn't ask what "arrangements" he had in mind. I craved feedback on my pantomime, but instead he stood up and escorted me to the door. Quivering, he mumbled that I shouldn't go back to work that afternoon but stay at home. I felt proud of clearly expressing some feelings deep within me.

When Kerstin came home from work, she was astonished to see me. I told her about our joint appointment with Dr. Lesser next morning, and it surprised me that she readily agreed to participate. Instead of sleeping, I spent the night roaming up and down the stairs, arranging and rearranging books in the their shelves, watching television, and poring over the notes on my book. An hour before dawn, Kerstin woke up and urged me to lie down and try to sleep. I furiously argued that I was fine and needed no sleep. As I still had to kill a couple of hours, I spent time outdoors, cleaning our backyard.

Once inside our townhouse, I pretended to be looking forward to the meeting, and spoke exuberantly of resuming work by noon. Kerstin looked tired and frightened. Her overt anxiousness bothered me, but I managed to restrain myself from shouting and waking up our neighbours.

Dr. Lesser spoke in a subdued voice as he explained to my wife that I was ill and hospital treatment was necessary. He then looked me in the eye and declared that a bed was awaiting me at the department of psychiatry at Sunnybrook Hospital. I accepted the news fatalistically, admitting to myself that I deserved whatever was happening. Somewhere deep inside I knew I was very sick and in need of medical treatment. I silently vowed to be a "good patient" at Sunnybrook and get discharged in a few days.

"What about my patients?" I asked.

"I'll call the hospital and tell them you'll be away from work indefinitely."

"Indefinitely" enraged me. It ran contrary to my plans, but I was very confused and incapable of expressing myself.

We took a cab to the emergency room of Sunnybrook Hospital, as my analyst had urged me not to drive. I spent hours waiting before a tall and slim resident examined me. I was in an extremely elated mood, and to amuse myself I answered all of his questions in great detail. Once the resident stopped asking questions, he reviewed some papers and announced that he was admitting me. After saying goodbye to my sobbing wife, I promised her I'd be home in a few days. She wiped her tears, and her face conveyed hurt and pain over my incapacity to understand how profoundly disturbed I was. A nurse escorted me to the adolescent wing of the department of psychiatry, as there were no beds available elsewhere. My good friend Harry visited me in that noisy ward the same evening. He sat next to me on my bed, his left eye slightly closed, peering into my eyes the way he vetted patients and colleagues that "just don't get it!" We chatted, but soon he looked amused as he said, "Tell me, boytchik, do you really believe it was by accident that you ended up in a ward jam-packed with teenagers?"

Though overwhelmed by that day's events, and unmistakably psychotic, I still managed to laugh feebly. Like ice water on a hot summer day, it revived me to hear a bit of kind-hearted flippancy in my dire circumstances.

"Yeah, Harry, I'm afraid you're right," I retorted, suddenly feeling sad. "It looks like I deserve to be locked up with kids. I can't deny I'm royally fucked-up!"

"Shalom," he said sternly, "people fall ill, people get well! As a psychologist, you know that. You'll be awhile on the ward. And once you're out, Peter Herschman, Alex

Dias, and myself will have at least seven assessments waiting for you to work on. Your reports are truly helpful, my friend."*

Though distractible, I managed somehow to calculate that seven assessments would bring in money enough to cover my bills for a month or so. And even more important, three colleagues I held in high esteem concurred that I wasn't incurably sick and would soon resume my work. I thanked Harry profusely for thinking of me. Next morning, a slim, ruddy-faced resident began assessing me. He pelted question after question at me, and I, pleased with myself, wanted to impress my assessor that we were bosom buddies jointly evaluating an obviously mild case. The resident didn't smile, and it infuriated me that he seemed worried about me. As he stood up from his chair, I flippantly asked, "So how do you feel about my hypomania?"

Lips puckered, he exclaimed, "Oh no, Shalom! It's a full-blown mania!"

That frightened me. Until that resident had spelled out my diagnosis, I had deluded myself that mine was a mild to moderate disorder. His directness burst my bubble of self-deception, and I began admitting to myself that I was

---

* Peter Herschman and Alex Dias were psychiatrists trained at the Menninger, who became psychoanalysts in Toronto. Quite often they referred to me, since Harry had recommended that I assess people likely to undergo psychoanalysis, or patients said to be difficult to treat.

sicker than I'd thought and conceded that it might take weeks, many weeks, before I could resume work.

The routines at the hospital were frightfully boring. I shaved and showered each morning, and after an unappetizing breakfast the nurse on call handed me a little white paper cup with medications: lithium, a mood stabilizer, and Stelazine, an antipsychotic. Further treatment consisted of daily occupational therapy, group therapy three times a week, a weekly meeting of all patients and staff, and daily chats with the nurse assigned to me. Despite the scheduled activities, each day I spent long hours doing nothing. To kill time, I paced the ward's long corridors, watched inane TV game shows, or scanned the newspapers and magazines Kerstin brought me every evening. In all, the tedium was excruciating, especially since my fellow patients on the ward were mixed-up teenagers with whom I had almost nothing in common.

Daily, I evaluated the impact each therapy had on me. At that stage of my treatment, I acted like a detached professional and a therapist, rather than a bona fide patient. After two weeks on the ward, I decided that I was well enough to be discharged. I notified my nurse of my intention, and my plan to be back at work the day after. She looked astonished and asked, "Are you well enough to be on your own, without hospital treatment?"

"Yes!" I replied vehemently, confident of having recovered. I knew that the staff could not keep me on the ward against my will, since I had entered the hospital voluntarily and was free to leave when I felt like. So I packed my bag, signed on a dotted line that I was leaving the hospital against medical advice, and headed home.

When Kerstin came back from work, she became furious when she saw me at home, even though she almost never got angry unless provoked by myself or her co-workers. My assertion that I was ready to leave Sunnybrook fell on deaf ears. She insisted that I wasn't well and needed to be in a hospital. I bellowed, "I feel betrayed! You show no faith in my capacity to have a life outside the abominable ward!"

As if to prove her right, I grabbed her throat. She somehow managed to wrest herself free and began scurrying around our dining room table, myself in pursuit and threatening her. Eventually, I tired from chasing her and went down to our basement to work on my book. For weeks I had neglected my research and felt pressured to resume writing. I skipped dinner, since I didn't want to hear my wife say that I was sick.

That evening I tried to read, but my concentration was again so poor that I barely took in the hundred-word abstracts of the articles I was studying. Furiously, I scribbled copious notes on psychotic versus nonpsychotic experiences in general, and on bipolar disorder in particular. I had some medication with me and chose to sleep on the living room sofa.

Next morning, I dressed up the way psychologists did in those days: a freshly ironed white shirt, a broad necktie, a navy-blue jacket, and grey pants. As I had woken up way too early, I killed time by scrubbing a few pairs of shoes with soap and water, then polishing them to a sheen.

By nine o'clock I sat in the waiting room by Bill's office, waiting to talk to my boss. When he approached me, I put forth my hand, but instead of shaking it, he cupped my elbow with his hand. I felt suspicious: Why was he so protective of me?

"Did my wife call you?" I asked Bill, suddenly worried that he too expected me to be in a psychiatric ward.

He let go of my elbow. "Why don't we talk in my office?" he said softly. "Patients may overhear us." He cocked his head to signify that I ought to follow him. Sitting behind his desk, Bill kept silent, waiting for me to say my piece.

I asked whether my wife had called him and he shook his head. "I'm ready to resume work," I declared. "I've been away for more than two weeks, and some patients might be upset."

"Don't worry," he said soothingly, "I took care of it. Your patients were notified of your illness."

"What did you tell them?" I barked menacingly.

"That you fell emotionally ill, and if they wanted to continue treatment, one of us in the psychology department would fill in for you."

The "emotionally ill" enraged me. Why couldn't he just say that I'd fallen ill, period? But I felt so eager to resume work that I feared that showing anger would be used against me.

"No one needs to fill in for me," I muttered. "I'm fit as a fiddle."

He leaned back against his chair, his chin raised. "Shalom, the hospital administration knows about your illness. It was decided that you'll come back to work only after Labour Day. The hospital was generous: you'll have a paid, four-month leave of absence."

My heart sank abruptly. Four months? Was that a punishment? I felt blood rushing to my face. "Who the fuck told the administration about my illness?" I yelled.

"I did." He leaned forward, his belly touching the desk. "You were psychotic before you entered Sunnybrook, and you need a lot of time to recover. Why don't you travel? Go to Israel! Take your wife to Sweden! Relax!"

Being called psychotic was worrisome. It's one thing to admit to yourself you're ill, quite another to be told that you are grossly dysfunctional and utterly crazy. I sat silent, in a rage, yet fearful of venting my feelings.

He stood up. "I have a patient waiting. I'll see you after Labour Day. Are you, by the way, seeing your therapist?"

I didn't reply. In my eagerness to go back to work, I'd entirely forgotten about my analysis. I pushed my chair back, stood up, and left Bill's office without saying a word. Only in the elevator going down to the lobby, my rage caught up with me. A powerful impulse took hold of me, and I felt like going back to my boss's office and hollering, "You're a fucking alcoholic! You called me psychotic, but you too were once hospitalized for a serious clinical depression! You have no right to call me psychotic! I hate you!"

Just as I had denied my mania by trumpeting that I was only hypomanic, I felt that being called psychotic rendered me vulnerable and hopelessly stigmatized. For days I wandered the streets, still buying books that I would lose on my way home. Once in our living room, I read for hours but absorbed very little. I hollered at my wife and children for no reason.

One day, as Kerstin repeated her view that I should return to the hospital, I flew into a rage and threatened to strangle her if she uttered another word. She left the room, and I felt terribly lonely.

In sheer desperation, I called T., a therapist I barely knew, who had recently arrived in Toronto from Israel. We met that same day, and I told her the "psychiatric authorities" and my wife were plotting against me, though I was completely sane. She naively believed I was a victim of persecution, and I saw a lot of her in the next few days. She invited me to her apartment, where I met her husband and teenage son.

In retrospect, T.'s harbouring me when I badly needed to be in a psychiatric ward actually did much harm. Well-meaning people at times take sides with the sick person, and instead of insisting that he take therapy, they shelter the alleged victim from his persecutors. That a mental health professional therapist failed to perceive how ill I was underscores how error-prone clinicians can be when they encounter the seriously ill.

Days later, Kerstin had tears of fear rolling down her cheeks as she begged me to return to the hospital. Again, I vehemently insisted that I needed no "incarceration." She implored me to return to Dr. Lesser, who had called to ask why I wasn't seeing him. I grabbed a long kitchen knife and threatened to kill her, and she fled upstairs and locked herself in the washroom.

Instantaneously, I resolved to take action and silence, once and for all, my wife and all those who thought me psychotic. I called 911 and hollered, "Retired Sergeant Shalom is ready!" I was in stitches when I added, "My wife will be serving you guys strong coffee and homemade buns—the Swedish way."

"Ready? What do you mean, Shalom?" a man's voice asked.

"I have a long Persian dagger deadlier than bayonets," I yelled. "I'll kill whoever tries to take me back to the loony bin."

"A hospital you mean? Which hospital, please?"

"Sunnybrook," I mumbled. "I left it a while ago. But I'm fine now."

"Are you married?"

"Yes I am, dummy! Don't you understand English? I told you my wife will be serving coffee and buns!" I paused to catch my breath. "She's driving me fucking crazy, my wife. She wants me locked up on the ward! I'll slice her like a turkey if she doesn't shut up! Do you understand?"

"What's your home address?"

I told him.

"Please put down the dagger and take it easy, Shalom. "We'll be there shortly. We'll talk to you and your wife. And we—"

I slammed the receiver down. Compelled by demons raging inside me, I ran to our bedroom. Out of the bottom drawer of our chest of drawers I pulled out a long antique Persian dagger, a gift from a dear friend I'd first met in the Israeli artillery.

I unsheathed the dagger and on my palm checked if its blade was pointy enough. Pleased, and growing more excited, I slid it back into its green leather sheath and tucked it into my belt. I ran down the stairs, stood by the window, and restlessly waited for the "dogcatchers" to come and get me.

As I waited, and my frenzy was escalating, I began to hallucinate Corporal Derzee, a Golani Brigade squad commander, booming at us recruits: "*Retzakh baeynayim*! *Retzakh baeynayim*!"—"Murder in your eyes!"—as he trained us to kill with a rifle-mounted bayonet. I was about to bark back at Derzee that I didn't hate Arabs and wasn't about to kill them, when I noticed two uniformed cops emerging from a cruiser parked in front of our townhouse. I hurried to the door, unlocked it, and in a moment heard their knocking on the door, so I hid behind a wall. One officer called my name, and I giggled, enjoying my exuberance to the hilt.

Soon I heard them open the door, close it softly, and wait by the entryway. Quit laughing, you moron, I chastised myself.

I heard them call my name again. Quickly, I turned around the wall hiding me and facing my foes I hollered, "Now!" And before they realized what I was up to, with a clenched fist I hit one of the dogcatchers hard in the gut, then kicked his groin. He bent over, moaning, and his partner fell a step back, noticeably frightened. Before he could react, I hurried to the door, swung it open, and found myself outdoors.

Without looking back, I began running through the driveways and alleys of our neighbourhood. I was in pretty good shape in those days, jogging five miles a week. Once out of breath I halted. I was now close to Bathurst and Steeles, an area with few housing developments at that time. I made sure I had my dagger firmly tucked under my belt. I looked about and saw no cruisers and no fiends in uniform. Without deliberating, I decided to flee to Montreal. To this day, I'm still in the dark as to why I resolved to hide in Montreal, of all places. It took me months to realize I was stark mad then, and all my thoughts and actions bizarre, erratic, and self-defeating.

It was rather cold that day, and before taking a cab to the airport, I bought an elegant black winter coat in a nearby men's store. The salesman helping me looked terrified when my dagger fell to the floor. He bent down and, hand trembling, handed me the weapon I loved so much.

I laughed hysterically and said, "I'll be using my baby if Montreal's dogcatchers mess with me!"

An hour later, I stood before an Air Canada agent at the airport, and bought a return ticket to Montreal. By mid-afternoon I arrived in Montreal and took a cab to a fine hotel. I called home several times, but there was no response. Worried, I prowled the streets in search for bookstores near the hotel. Eventually, I found myself in Old Montreal, where I dined on frogs' legs and expensive wine. In my rusty French, I kidded with the waiter who remained stern and unsmiling throughout. He looked perplexed when I asked if he sold dictionaries and thesauruses on the side. "To me," I forcefully insisted, "you come across as a Gallic intellectual working part-time in a restaurant to make ends meet." Seemingly determined not to smile, he remarked that bookstores would open next morning, at ten. I left him a huge tip.

Back in the hotel, I tried to read the Bible I had discovered in the drawer of my bedside table. My concentration was so poor that I only managed to read the opening paragraphs of Genesis. Several times I called home, but no one answered. About midnight I ordered over the phone a bottle of expensive red wine. Minutes later, I heard a knock on the door, and once I opened it, I saw a moustached waiter staring at me. I joked with him in French and English, and he laughed. I gave him a twenty-dollar tip, saying, "I really appreciate your warmth and empathy." As he laughed with abandon, I concluded that the waiter was part of a benevolent, worldwide conspiracy to make me feel safe and protected.

I gulped down the red wine as if it were orange juice and soon felt tipsy. Without undressing, I fell asleep on the bed. Next morning I woke up with an awful hangover. I called home several times, but got no answer. Just as I had arbitrarily decided to hide in Montreal, on a whim I decided to fly back to Toronto. The journey home scared me because I remembered the dogcatchers' determination to get even with me.

In the afternoon I arrived at our empty home. Only weeks later, having sufficiently recovered, did Kerstin reveal that, after I'd attacked the police officer, she'd taken the children to the home of a friend. Harry visited her and said that nothing could be done until I ran myself ragged and would, on my own, seek readmission to Sunnybrook Hospital. Things turned out pretty much as Harry had predicted. I spent an hour at home rifling through Bibles and books while absorbing nothing, until an insufferable loneliness descended upon me. I ordered a cab for Sunnybrook Hospital. On the way, I concocted a luminous scenario of myself being welcomed at the hospital as a great man returning to a location where he was venerated.

I have no particular memories of being readmitted other than being placed in an isolation cell with a green iron door. There was a bed bolted to the floor and a small window close to the ceiling with three thick iron bars. I began venting rage by bellowing cuss words, kicking the door, then tearing up the mattress with teeth and nails. My protest ended with pounding on the windowpane with a shoe till it cracked.

The response was swift. Three male nursing aides came into the room, easily subdued me, and into my buttock gave me a shot of Haldol, a widely used antipsychotic. I calmed down considerably, even before the drug fully kicked in, so impressed was I by the effectiveness of the Goliaths on staff. For many days I had been dangerously out of control, and being forced to contain my rage struck me as something beneficial, even then.

The next morning, a fearful-looking resident pronounced me calm enough to leave the isolation cell. That same day I joined regular hospital treatment and benefitted mostly from group therapy. Weeks later, the staff psychiatrist in charge of my treatment expressed amazement at my slow progress. "I can't discharge you!" he exclaimed, like a judge hammering down a verdict. "If you were a carpenter, there would be no problem with you going home now. But you're a psychologist, you treat people, and I don't think I can trust you yet."

I flinched, as I didn't yet understand what was so terribly wrong with me. How can I change my conduct, I asked myself, when I have no idea in what ways I'm out of line?

After five weeks in hospital, it was decided that I had recovered enough to be discharged. True, I had been admitted voluntarily, and could have left the hospital had I wanted to. But this time I listened to the staff and waited until they concluded that I had improved enough and was capable of going home and working.

On a Friday afternoon I arrived home and waited for my wife and children, my heart beating fast and painfully. I was aching to resume the life I'd had prior to my upsets and debacles. The house was clean and tidy, but I decided to look at our garage. Once I opened its door, the mess overwhelmed me. Kerstin didn't have a driver's licence in those days, and a layer of grey dust covered our green Volvo. The floor was littered with tools my sons had used but neglected to put back in the tool box. The shelves I'd spent long hours installing were in disarray, and that hurt me the most. The chaotic, dirty garage was, in my eyes, emblematic of my disordered life in the last few months. Guilt and profound sadness came over me, but I was determined not to succumb, and right away I started cleaning and mending the garage and, indirectly, my shattered life.

The following Monday morning I met with Dr. Lesser. I sat on a chair, since he had announced that I would no longer be in analysis and would be seeing him twice a week. He went on to say that when he visited me in the hospital he noticed how attached I was to the female nurses. I found that comment useless, even stupid, but I decided not to reply, as I had little confidence in him, and I welcomed having less frequent appointments.

Without an aura or a warning, I began to sob as deeply as if an iceberg deep inside had totally melted down. I wept and wept, and the more I sobbed the more curative the weeping felt. When the crying ended, I told him that his visiting me in the hospital had put me in touch with bottomless hurt and resentment over the few colleagues that ever visited me on the ward. I complained of feeling abysmally sorry for myself.

Looking back, it was evident that my colleagues had no inkling about how to relate to a colleague who had become starkly disturbed. Were they scared? Tongue-tied? Inhibited? Afraid of contagion? Or were they mediocrities incapable of taking the risk involved in handling situations they hadn't been trained or supervised on? They hated and felt threatened by my pre-morbid busyness inside and outside the hospital; they ignored my suffering and thought that I'd made my bed and time had come for me to lie in it. Mental health professionals do not treat a colleague gone mad warmly. Only gifted clinicians, like Harry Hardin, Peter Herschman, and a few others, had what it took to react spontaneously and empathetically to an outright insane member of their profession. My lay friends were kinder and more accepting of my illness than the vast majority of my colleagues. It was quite obvious that far too many therapists clung to the belief that they're more rational, more insightful than their charges—a laughable myth, given that so many therapists have sexually abused their patients. Also, therapists as a group are the most eager consumers of years-long psychotherapy, which militates against any self-congratulatory illusions of being immune to mental illnesses.

From May until Labour Day that year I did no clinical work. The only exception was a psychotherapy group I co-led with a friend, Aris Slesers. He was then a psychiatrist at St. Michael's Hospital, and we had been co-therapists of a group for over a year. Aris was not at all intimidated by my illness and trusted my capacity to work with patients. This was the only professional work I did during those months, as all the private patients I had seen prior to my breakdown had vanished while I was ill. I spent my abundant free time reading, walking, and taking care of our home. Those months taught me how to spend time meaningfully, but without acting like a workaholic, as I had done before my collapse.

Were the years of exuberance, high energy, and enthusiasm signs and symptoms of a disease? I asked myself. Was I seriously disturbed even before I became overtly psychotic? Such tangled conundrums may one day become understood thanks to methodologically sound research. Only empirical investigations, and not brilliant speculations, will show us humans the way out of the mazes we have been born into, or those we have inadvertently corralled ourselves into.

Chapter 5

A Second Interlude

I RESUMED WORK AT THE HOSPITAL THE TUESDAY after Labour Day and straightaway made profound changes to my work. First, I stopped treating schizophrenics in group therapy. That line of work is so emotionally consuming that my friends advised me to let go of it completely. With their help, I realized that I must protect myself from my own excesses.

Equally painful was putting an end to my research on schizophrenic people. I shredded all of my notes and many pages of text as I resolved never to resume that inquiry. Deciding not to write a magnum opus felt like waking up from a night-long nightmare.

I took up new, less demanding challenges, such as taking workshops on hypnosis. I read profusely on the topic and acquired considerable clinical experience. In turn, this boosted my brittle self-confidence.

The romance with hypnotherapy, however, lasted less than three years. I began noticing that those benefitting from hypnosis were faithful converts that staunchly believed they not only would be cured of all symptoms but would live as happily as a newborn nursed by his mother. I had previously observed a similar phenomenon: how converts to psychoanalysis expected their analyses to bring about a perfectly happy existence, not merely relieve them of pain and suffering. And, by 2001, clinical experience led me to conclude that patients who insisted on having nothing but cognitive behaviour therapy benefitted from it much more than those who had never heard of it. Since religions are found in virtually every culture, we humans seem to be hardwired to embrace some form of faith—even secular ones such as communism, atheism, psychoanalysis, or cognitive therapy.

My work at the hospital also changed. I was now supervised by a staff psychiatrist who claimed he was not really supervising me, since I was experienced enough and did good work. I ignored that assertion, as I had decided to stop confronting people in authority. I no longer took on patients said to be "difficult," as I had eagerly done before I fell ill. I was resolved to take it easy, and like my colleagues I slowly built a private practice, treating people likely to benefit from psychotherapy. I saw a psychiatrist for twenty minutes every other week, to check the impact of the drugs I was taking on my functioning.

Life went on smoothly, as I refrained from obsessing about the inevitable recurrence of malignant mood swings. In fact, a psychiatrist I was friendly with asked if I had experienced bouts of melancholia after my breakdown. I said I had not, but his question jolted me. Was it a law of nature that hideous moods would assail me again and again? Was I so out of order that psychic torments were likely to reoccur?

Before I found reasonable answers to such quandaries, I noticed some perturbing changes in Dr. Lesser's behaviour. He was late for appointments, and once when I came to see him in his suite he was not there. His speech became loud and hard to follow, and he appeared restless and unkempt. Though usually soft-spoken, now he would interrupt me harshly, and often it seemed as if he had not been listening.

These changes frightened me because I worried about his sanity—and mine. I spoke with Dr. Pinsker, the chief of psychiatry, about Dr. Lesser's behaviour, since he was a consultant at the hospital. Dr. Pinsker thanked me for my openness and vowed to discuss my concerns with my analyst. Days later, my analyst's secretary called to inform me that he would be away for a while and would call me as soon as he returned to work. I asked my colleagues at the hospital what was going on, but I met walls of silence everywhere I turned. Eventually, I asked Harry Hardin what the hell was happening, and he admitted to taking Stan Lesser to a hospital in New York with the aid of another analyst. "Don't worry," he told me, "he will recover soon. You are not going to lose him."

"What's the matter with him?" I asked demandingly.

"You can ask him when he's back. He'll let you know."

"I'm not sure I want to continue with him," I erupted. "No matter how sick I was at the time, I did all I could not to let my illness perturb my patients. I may, no doubt, have hurt some of them, but Stan Lesser was so erratic, so crazy at work, that his madness disturbed me!"

"Shalom," Harry said in an avuncular tone, "people fall ill, people get better and you—"

"I know all that, Harry!"

"Dr. Lesser will be back," Harry continued, unflappable. "He'll explain himself, and you'll resume your therapy with him."

"Who are you trying to protect, Harry?" I charged, raring to have a fight. "Him or me? Are you his friend or mine?"

"I'm your friend, and I'm trying to reassure you that your analyst will be all right. He's in good hands and soon he'll be with you."

That exchange did not reassure me. Harry was approaching the problem as a psychoanalyst: what mattered most was my relationship with my therapist, and my supposed fear of losing him in particular. But what angered me most was my analyst's illness impinging on his work. In my rather distorted view, I clung to the idea that even while manic I had performed adequately at work, a questionable assumption. As madness progressed, I couldn't help my overexcitement and had pressured some patients to make rapid changes to their behaviour. Lacking empathy, I had "forgotten" that only people on the verge of a psychosis make abrupt and drastic changes to their identity. People in therapy change aspects of their personality or alter their lifestyle slowly, over months, or even years. My past eagerness to have my patients speed up their recovery was, in my eyes, less disruptive than my analyst's utter disorganization at work.

My wife had an access of anger upon hearing how my analyst had been whisked away to New York to receive treatment. "You're not a psychiatrist! You're not a psychoanalyst!" she blared out. "So you were treated as a second-rate patient and were allowed to act crazy for months." I didn't reply because I was then too upset to start a fight.

After being away for a month, Dr. Lesser called to let me know he was now back at work. When I met with him, he looked ashen-faced and noticeably slimmer. His eyes were grave and stern, suggesting a steely determination to resume his life prior to his breakdown. I empathized with this stance, as his face reminded me of how I had felt the day I returned to work after a four-month absence. There was, I felt, a supreme irony in two manic-depressive therapists endeavouring to maintain a semblance of normality.

My anger petered out slowly as I observed Dr. Lesser's efforts to ensure that his world was in order. I felt sorry for his illness and humiliation, his pretending that his life was now under control and his madness unlikely to reoccur soon. I told him how I'd warned Dr. Pinsker about his odd behaviour. Instead of expressing gratitude, he asked me how I felt about his being away for a month. I remembered how after my mania he'd advised me not to apologize to my patients; he was, indeed, practising what he'd preached to me, and that put me at ease. I briefly mentioned my upset about his month-long absence, but I didn't mention my fury about him fouling his own nest because I was afraid of hurting him badly.

Only after I was no longer in therapy with him did I realize that my analyst had, just like me, experienced a full-blown manic episode. Just as I had initially minimized the extent of my illness, it took time before I realized the depth of *his* psychosis. I had witnessed his disorganization, but I refrained from affixing adjectives like "manic" or "psychotic" to him. I was his patient and needed him to be resourceful, strong, able to help me, and in charge of my treatment.

A therapist's capacity to help cannot be doubted by his patients—one of the reasons I never told any of my patients about my bipolar disorder. I invariably lied about my sudden absences from work, and informed those in treatment with me that I had been away for health reasons, without ever mentioning what disease I was struggling with.

For decades I was totally convinced that my mere mention of my bipolar disorder would end my professional career, as my patients would reject out of hand a mentally ill psychologist. While some progress has been made against the stigmatization of the mentally ill, the notion of being in therapy with a mentally disordered healer is still not something the public may tolerate. And I don't see this changing in the near future. I began writing this memoir now that I am largely retired, with relatively little to lose if some patients find out I have periodically been psychotic. After concealing my illness for decades, concealment became a way of life for me, my wife, and my children. And yet I resolved to end the conspiracy of silence. Better late than never, I said to myself, to allay my regrets over not coming out of the closet sooner.

After Dr. Lesser resumed work, I continued therapy with him for a few months. But I derived little benefit as I wondered whether he was still ill, and, just like me, systematically camouflaging it. I suspected that throughout my analysis he was grieving his wife and was probably unable to provide me with whatever I needed. When I fell gravely ill, he mismanaged my manic episode because his bipolar disorder caused immense fears, I suppose, and rendered him ineffective.

After all is said and done, I feel Dr. Lesser's therapeutic impact on me was much less than Dr. Tamarin's. The latter gave me hell quite often, but I always sensed how important it was to him that I take initiatives that would lead my family and me to enjoy life as much as possible. Dr. Lesser, on the other hand, failed to realize how morbidly elated

I was getting by the day; he arranged for me to enter a hospital only when I became so unmistakably psychotic that any lay person would have firmly pointed out that I belonged in a psychiatric ward.

From mid-1977 to mid-1981, I was free of overt symptoms of bipolar disorder. Those were good years, as I developed a part-time private practice, and, once laid off from Mount Sinai Hospital, I became a self-employed psychologist in private practice. Friends and colleagues that knew of my illness still referred their patients to me, especially for group and marital therapy. I let them know I was seeing a psychiatrist regularly, and informed them about my hospitalizations. They probably realized I was a compliant, responsible doctor-cum-patient they could trust. As well, my family life was developing well. We bought a small house in a fine neighbourhood, where my wife and children felt comfortable.

Chapter 6

Mood Swings and Manias

IN 1981, WHEN I TURNED FORTY-TWO, SYMPTOMS OF serious melancholia unexpectedly came over me. My moods were exasperatingly low, I felt sluggish and experienced few pleasures. I became dissatisfied with my life, even though just months before I had felt reasonably content and happy. But there was nothing dramatic about those moods, unlike the ones I went through in Israel. Though I ruminated a great deal, I no longer suffered from delusions of becoming destitute, and did not regard myself a failure. My practice, for example, kept growing slowly. I deceived myself by affirming that I was going through a neurotic depression—a mild depression of sorts, not necessarily a manifestation of bipolar illness. Deceiving oneself, by the way, is not unique to people with bipolar disorder but a characteristic of humanity in general.

I shared with Harry Hardin my need to see a psychotherapist about my discomforting feelings. He said I ought to see Dr. Lesser again, but I vehemently refused. He then referred me to Eugene Mandryk, a psychiatrist Harry described as a fine psychotherapist he had supervised for five years.

Unlike Dr. Tamarin and Dr. Lesser, Dr. Mandryk assessed me methodically and thoroughly over a period of several weeks—a practice Harry had inculcated in him. Dr. Mandryk concluded that my difficulties handling my two growing sons had triggered the current dysphoria, and he recommended family therapy for the four of us. I rejected his recommendation because my condition had worsened. He kindly agreed to take me on as a patient in psychotherapy.

At the time I started therapy, Dr. Mandryk must have been forty-five. He was of Ukrainian descent, a handsome man and a sharp dresser. His eyes were dark brown, his cheeks slightly ruddy, and his thick brown hair was meticulously combed. His tastefully decorated office included a consulting room with two Eames chairs, with a black leather ottoman between them, so that both doctor and patient could rest their feet on the ottoman.

Though I saw Dr. Mandryk once a week for almost five years, I have little to say about him. Unlike Dr. Tamarin, there was nothing flamboyant about him, and I can't recall any memorable interventions coming from him. He was a hard-working, conscientious therapist, who did his best to help me. He was such an effective journeyman that I wish a helpful psychotherapist like him could treat all emotionally troubled people.

Only at the end of our work together did he begin showing signs of distress. Once or twice his eyes rolled as if he were having difficulty keeping them open. I stopped talking when this happened, and he broke the silence. "I'm having some stress in my life," he said unapologetically, indicating that his life was not a bed of roses at all times.

Days later, I saw him seated in the large waiting room I shared with eight other psychotherapists in my building. He was, apparently, waiting for his therapist. He greeted me unabashedly, with no apparent concern. As he later explained, ten years earlier he had been in analysis, and now that he was experiencing stress, he went back to his analyst for a "tune-up." The need for therapy was handled spontaneously, as he apparently believed I would understand him and pass no harsh judgment. His conduct somehow reminded me of Ruth Easser, the analyst who had first introduced me to the world of therapists that did not hide behind clever theories, platitudes, and buzzwords.

Dr. Mandryk helped me greatly in dealing with the vicissitudes of private practice. Initially, I experienced difficulties in the transition from working as a staff psychologist in a hospital to the role of sole practitioner. Personally, I preferred the security of a regular, biweekly paycheque to the freedoms of self-employment, such as coming and going as you please. In those days, I worried whenever there were openings in my work schedule, which made my income hard to predict. Dr. Mandryk reassured me that I was doing fine, and my anxiety over the loss of a regular paycheque was entirely understandable. He had a way of referring to "we psychotherapists" that was very reassuring. I often felt that we were both in the same boat, perhaps having similar worries. I liked him and his style, and was grateful for his many efforts on my behalf.

His insistence that I could function as a private practitioner was not only helpful and reassuring but also prophetic. In the decades to come, whether depressed or hypomanic, I disguised, rather successfully, my disorder behind a front of engaging in a solo clinical practice. Were I a salaried therapist working in an agency or clinic, I would have to attend team meetings, where my less-than-optimal functioning would be more easily noted. But as a self-employed practitioner, all I needed was to perform well for fifty minutes in individual psychotherapy, and for an hour and a half in group therapy. I covered up my occasional dysfunction by assuming the role of attentive listener who remembered practically everything my patients had divulged. In all the years I treated patients while I was, at times, sicker than they were, only one patient ever complained openly about my infrequent absent-mindedness. He regarded my distractibility as an amusing quirk that made him laugh, not a manifestation of serious dysfunction.

Of necessity, I had to be good at concealing my disorder. At one point, while moderately depressed, my caseload included a couple of psychiatrists, one psychologist, and a social worker. And yet I heard no complaints from professionals trained to detect psychopathology, and some of them even recommended me to their colleagues. As stated, the role psychotherapists play is one of the safest. Patients pour their hearts out to a sympathetic listener who decides how much—or how little—to disclose of himself. I dissembled my condition by actively participating in dialogues and group sessions even on days when I was quite alarmingly depressed. And while hypomanic, I would constrain my gesticulations by sitting on my splayed hands—literally—and letting patients carry the ball. But in group therapy, where a therapist's shortcomings may be noted by a small audience, the leader feels more exposed and vulnerable. I learned that too much commotion and laughter in group sessions were sure signs I was becoming pathologically elated.

My adamant pursuit of a predictable life, such as working five days a week and actively participating in family life, helped me a lot. And once I took up creative writing I enjoyed a sense of direction and purpose that made my life meaningful and worthwhile. Slowly, my stories were accepted for publication and I felt that my literary efforts were appreciated. I defined myself as a psychologist first and a writer second, and my modest accomplishments strengthened my resolve never to surrender to debilitating symptoms.

Personal problems rarely happen in isolation. There are always numerous issues and troubles contending for attention and limited emotional resources. Thus, while struggling with harrowing moods, my son Daniel was giving his parents a very hard time. From an early age he had been rebellious and disobedient, and his teachers repeatedly complained about his restlessness and pranks. In high school, the vice-principal frequently complained about our son's outrageous conduct that drew attention from teachers and peers. Socially, he was very popular, and his friends often called him, so that he was on the phone for hours. My wife and I tried to reason with him but failed, as he enjoyed defying all manner of authority figures. One evening, when Daniel was fourteen, he came home from a party very intoxicated. He soon began drinking beer heavily, and our pleas for restraint made no impact on him. "I really *don't* like the taste of beer or liquor," he told me years later, when he admitted to being an alcoholic. "I love what booze does to me. It makes me feel high and funny—the life of the party."

I avoided confrontations with Daniel because he angered me so much that I dreaded losing control and hitting him. Thus, I let my kind-hearted, softie wife deal with school principals and whoever complained about our son. I believe my son was cognizant of my underlying rage, since he was very perceptive and quick to figure out others' unexpressed feelings.

While pathologically elated, I would shout at Daniel and my wife. Mine were rages born of impotence, and while disordered I experienced few boundaries. I hollered almost indiscriminately, and my ranting stopped only when I became physically exhausted. Kerstin and my sons knew, of course, that my outbursts were sick and dreaded them. Martin, our first-born, stayed out of my way and never provoked me.

My depression, meanwhile, had worsened, and the prescribed antidepressants were not doing me any good. My deteriorating moods worried me a great deal, and I felt so sluggish that it took me a lot of effort to walk ten minutes. A crushing sense of despair came over me, although I couldn't specify what I was despaired about, and once again I contemplated suicide. I shared those thoughts with Dr. Mandryk, and he observed that they were manifestations of my illness. What I withheld was my stashing away medication to overdose on it, and thus rid myself of severe mood swings and incessant despair. One day, Dr. Mandryk remarked that he was concerned about my facial expression. "Your eyes are very dim," he said, "almost deadened. It's a sign of serious depression. You need aggressive treatment."

"But I'm functioning well at work," I muttered, worried about the concept of "aggressive treatment." "Yes, I suffer a lot at home and at work," I added, "but I can handle it."

"But you're not sleeping enough," he riposted. "At night you walk up and down the stairs for hours. You're suicidal and you look agitated right now. I'm considering ECT."

I shuddered. Electroconvulsive treatment? Shock treatment, in plain English. I pictured myself in greenish hospital robes, tethered to a gurney, and convulsing uncontrollably. "No!" I shouted. "I'm afraid of memory loss. ECT is too dangerous! It won't help me!"

Dr. Mandryk benevolently shook his head. "You psychologists are biased against it. It's a benign and humane therapy. As for memory loss, it's a thing of the past, when people received dozens of treatments. You'll probably have less than ten."

"I don't want it!" I cried out. "I'm terrified! I'd rather continue with medication and psychotherapy." In truth, I was twenty pills short of the sixty I needed for a lethal dose.

Dr. Mandryk leaned forward. "I'll refer you to Dr. Emmanuel Persad, an expert on ECT. Let's see what he has to say about medication and ECT." I felt numb, the prospect of shock treatments more frightening than overdosing.

I called Dr. Persad, and days later I sat in his corner office at the Clarke Institute of Psychiatry. He was a swarthy, middle-aged man with greying temples. His ultra-tidy desk suggested a cerebral, well-organized man.

He took notes on a yellow, lined pad as I answered his questions. I wondered, "Is he, perhaps, more interested in keeping neat records than in understanding me?" Still, he continued to fire question after question about my illness and the various medications I'd taken. He paused, gave me a long once-over, and in a surprisingly soothing voice said, "You're very ill. You suffer from manic-depressive illness."

Manic-depressive illness, I anxiously asked myself. Over the years I'd accepted the idea that I'd had a manic break and that horrendous depressions had come my way. And yet this was the first time I'd ever heard the words "manic" and "depressive" being cobbled together to denote a single disease entity.

Flabbergasted, I stared at Dr. Persad. "I must have been in denial," I imploringly said. "For years I've been aware of being ill, and yet I didn't admit to the gravity and the precise nature of my illness. But the way you phrased it made some walls inside me come tumbling down."

"Dr. Mandryk is right," he summed up. "ECT will help. You are on the verge of a severe psychosis, and we must arrest it."

As I said nothing, he continued. "Read Norman Endler's book, *Holiday of Darkness*. Like you, he is a psychologist with manic-depressive illness. Initially, he was afraid of ECT because he had once observed a patient convulse horribly when she got the old form of the treatment. Talk to him. Tell him I gave you his name."

Despite my impaired concentration, I managed to read much of Endler's book. I called him, and we met in his office at York University. It turned out he was a researcher, not a clinician. He gave me no advice but shared with me that ECT had greatly helped him.

After meeting Dr. Endler I agreed to have ECT. There was nothing dramatic or lurid about it. One late afternoon, I checked into the Wellesley Hospital and was told that the first treatment would be administered the next morning. Before breakfast I was asked to lie on a gurney, and an attendant wheeled me through the corridors until we reached a large room. A man in a white lab coat introduced himself as the psychiatrist in charge and asked me if I had any questions. I mumbled that Dr. Mandryk had prepared me for the treatment, and I needed no further explanations.

My recollection of ECT itself is blurry and indistinct. I recall an anaesthetist giving me an injection, and the psychiatrist fiddling with his equipment. Next I remember lying on a gurney, back on the psychiatry ward. I was in a daze and confused but didn't feel any different from the day before.

Altogether, I had nine treatments, three a week, when I was forty-four years old. After each treatment I was free to do as I pleased. It was excruciatingly boring having to spend three weeks on the ward. My wife and children were on vacation in Sweden, since Dr. Mandryk saw no need to cancel their trip. My friend Peter Herschman visited me several times, and I received a lot of warm support from him and his wife, Pat.

I had ardent hopes that ECT would entirely dissipate my serious depression. But this is a common daydream: distraught people expect a total erasure of all their symptoms, rather than a slow, gradual, and realistic improvement.

Nothing miraculous happened to me. My mood remained low, and I felt numb and discouraged. The only noticeable relief was the disappearance of suicidal ideations. When I expressed my disappointment to Dr.

Mandryk, he said that the ECT had helped me "get over the hump." He was right, though I didn't notice it at the time. Within weeks I dumped into the garbage the dozens of antidepressants I had hoarded.

Despite George Orwell's dire prophesies, 1984 was, for me, a rather good year. I was symptom-free and felt alive and energetic. My practice was growing, and I billed more hours than ever. I presented a workshop on leading experiential workshops at an international convention of group psychotherapists, where my recommendations were well received. Not only was I in an acceptable mood but also our finances were in good shape and delusions of poverty were, in my eyes, a thing of the past.

Chapter 7

Rapid Cycling

PEOPLE WITH BIPOLAR DISORDER ARE SAID TO BE rapid cycling when they experience four or more mood swings in one year. The rapid cycling may be extreme, such as mood swings occurring in a few days, or, very rarely, even on the same day. The latter is nothing but hell on earth, and those experiencing frequent and extreme mood changes report feeling incapacitated and confused about their identity. Once, while hospitalized at the Clarke Institute, I met a patient whose moods swung several times a day. He was not an articulate person, and I asked him numerous questions before I grasped how genuinely infernal his life was. He lived in a small town in northern Ontario and suffered immensely because, wherever he turned, he was called crazy.

Once, while rapid cycling, I became very manic. I began ranting so incoherently that my son Martin, usually a stoic and composed boy, burst out crying. Dr. Mandryk arranged for me to be admitted to the psychiatry ward at Etobicoke General Hospital. My wife drove me there, but on the way I yelled incessantly at her, and since she adamantly refused to drive me back home, I grabbed hold of the steering wheel and the car dangerously veered right and left.

At the hospital, I was given a heavy dose of an antipsychotic that soon quietened my loud ranting; I was relatively calm and lucid the next morning. The unceasing advances in drug therapy made it possible to bring down my overexcited ranting and raving in a matter of days, sometimes within hours.

An experienced therapist can continue practising despite a severe bipolar disorder, provided he checks into a hospital when his condition alarmingly deteriorates. In this respect, the doctor-cum-patient needs much support and guidance from family, therapists, colleagues, and friends. It was my wife's persistence and my doctors' urging me not to capitulate but keep on striving that enabled me to lead a modest life with a few professional and literary accomplishments.

One Monday stands out clearly. I had spent several days in a hospital, was discharged on a Sunday afternoon, and resumed work the next morning. I saw several patients throughout the morning and early afternoon, and was scheduled to co-lead a group with Aris Slesers, who was aware of my recent hospitalization. I had encountered only minor difficulties conducting the individual therapy sessions and looked forward to the group experience.

That day, Aris and I were scheduled to lead our group behind a one-way mirror, so that therapists in training could observe us leading a group session. The session over, we had a discussion with the trainees about the afternoon's session. Aris and I had worked together for over eight years and our performance that afternoon was flawless. The trainees fired off questions, and they theorized on what the leaders had done and what had transpired in the course of therapy. While reviewing the group session, I conducted myself relatively well, and no trainee appeared to have noticed that my psychiatric condition had very recently been much worse than my patients'.

It's fortunate that I recover from manic states almost as quickly as I get into them. But some of my manias were so incapacitating that it took me weeks to recover, especially in earlier years, when antipsychotics were less curative than they are nowadays. The treatment of my depressions, however, was much less effective. Only by 2010, when I was seventy-one, were my godawful mood swings brought under pharmacological control.

Months prior to my rapid cycling, George Boujoff, a distinguished, humorous analyst, referred to me a young psychiatrist and his wife for marital therapy. George, like me, regarded any therapist's prolonged immersion in his own neuroses—countertransference—as an indication of festering narcissism. I was then functioning quite well, and the couple liked my no-nonsense handling of the therapy sessions. A while later, the husband gave my name to a friend of his, a psychiatrist, who also began attending therapy with his wife. Yet, months later, when I became gravely ill, I began to dread the two psychiatrists, since I had persuaded myself that they would notice how horrendously depressed I had become and summarily fire me.

Nothing like that happened. The two psychiatrists never seemed to notice the changes in my moods, and continued their therapy for many months. As pointed out, conducting psychotherapy is a very protected role, and a well-trained and sufficiently supervised therapist can hide almost all of his symptoms behind the studied façade of "socially designated healer."

While approaching mania, I was often unaware of how disturbed my supercharged moods were. One could say that, while manic, I experienced life as an unceasing, everlasting party that I enjoyed to the hilt, but my family's pain and distress then were enormous. On the other hand, when severe depressions afflicted me, I suffered immensely, but my family felt they could continue living with me since I had no outbursts of rage while depressed.

Truth be told, I was more often hypomanic—half-mad, in plain words—rather than totally deranged and manic. While morbidly elated, I was somewhat aware of my condition, as the therapies I took had taught me to recognize when I was inching toward disabling psychotic states. Yet I frequently enjoyed my hypomanias, since they made me feel creative and talented, although, once recovered, the ideas I had entertained while hypomanic often struck me as dismissible megalomania or outright gibberish.

But the chief target of my rages was my wife. More than once I threatened to kill her, and even ran after her with a knife. Only my love for her when I was not psychotic contained my dangerous, murderous impulses. Perhaps, unbelievably, even while enraged and violence-prone, I did love her and remained grateful to her, though in a distorted, pathological manner. More than once I was just about to throttle her to death, when her frightened eyes reminded me that I loved her, and I would let go.

Once, I noticed, to my astonishment, that some of my books had swastikas drawn on them. I became upset and hurt, since two of my grandparents and dozens of close relatives had been murdered in Auschwitz and Treblinka. Many times I had shared with my sons my intense, uncompromising hatred for Nazis and Nazism. They knew I was reluctant to buy goods produced in Germany, my furious boycott of Wagner's music was unwavering and uncompromising, and I vowed never to set foot on German soil. Those swastikas felt like betrayal. My initial response was to do nothing. (Some abusers rage at minor issues but defeat themselves by suppressing legitimate hurt and ire.) I asked my sons who had drawn the swastikas, and my fifteen-year-old Daniel right away admitted to it. "Daniel," I spoke in a slow, measured voice, "how come you drew Nazi symbols on my books? You know very well how I feel about anything Nazi!" I was moderately depressed at the time and chastising my son was a difficult thing to do.

"It was a joke," he answered, his eyes conveying dread of me hollering, perhaps even beating him up. Days before, I'd had an outburst of rage because Daniel had used some tools of mine but, as always, had left them strewn on the living room floor.

"A joke?" I peered at him icily, an executioner peering at the man he was about to kill. "A joke? With Nazi emblems? At home?" As I had not yet exploded, some of my son's dread had dissipated.

"It didn't mean anything, Dad," he retorted. "They were just stupid drawings."

"But many of my books bear swastikas," I raised my voice. "It wasn't a single instance."

Now he looked irate, and the supposed trifles I was bringing up were annoying him. All his life Daniel had resented my authority, and my calling him to task was angering him. "So let's say, Dad, that you don't like my sense of humour."

"But Daniel," I said imploringly, my spinelessness bothering not only me but him too. "We are Jews. Don't you know what the Nazis did to our family, to six million of us?"

"Of course, I know! No need to rub it in!" Though angry, he spoke softly, probably recalling my frequent rages. "I meant no disrespect, Dad. As I said, it was just a joke."

"Did you draw swastikas on school books?"

"Of course not! It's not the same thing! They wouldn't get the point!"

Suddenly, I felt unable to further pursue the conversation. Over the years, the swastikas continued to hurt me. I felt alienated from my son, and in moments of rage—no shortages of those—I would feel belittled and betrayed. Despite my efforts to put my feelings in perspective, such as accepting that my son was rebellious and impetuous, I had a hard time forgiving him.

Whenever I encountered signs of Daniel's excessive drinking, I would invariably resent those swastikas. I felt persecuted, no matter how many times I said to myself that Daniel was just a child defying his father's authority. Years after I had discovered that some of my books had been violated, a Jewish friend of mine let me know that one of his teenage sons had painted swastikas on the wall of the synagogue the family infrequently attended. This story confirmed my suspicion that Daniel's drawings were not acts of hatred but of rebellion. A swastika was guaranteed to draw attention.

One morning, I woke up feeling disturbingly odd, and minutes later I began complaining about our home being dark and gloomy. True, we lived in a sixty-year-old house with little daylight coming in, but I was, no doubt, experiencing a major disturbance, and the low light in our home was just an excuse to vent rage. I felt restless and, on utter impulse, went shopping for compact discs, a technological novelty in those days. It was an entirely irrational idea, since at the time we owned no CD player.

I must have been quite psychotic when I entered a music store not far from our home. I took an immediate liking for the cute-looking discs, though in 1985 the number of discs featuring classical music was quite limited. I held a shopping basket and filled it up completely with discs whose covers I didn't bother to read. It occurred to me to pilfer the discs, so I hid the basket under the trench coat I was wearing. That was a stupid way of stealing, as the coat hardly concealed the shopping basket. A store clerk approached me and bumptiously asked how he could help me. I flared up, irate that the clerk had figured out my ruse. Mumbling curses, I paid for the entire collection of CDs, which I hid in two of my desk's drawers.

A week later, my wife returned what I called "my loot" to the store, claiming we had no CD player, and that I had acted strangely because of mental illness. The store owner took back the merchandise and told Kerstin that he clearly remembered me. "Your husband behaved strangely," he said. "He hid the discs under his coat, then readily paid for them, as though he couldn't wait to get home and listen to them."

Days later, Kerstin and I agreed to see *Kiss of the Spider Woman*, a movie with Sonia Braga, a Brazilian actress I liked. While waiting for dinner, I remembered, out of the blue, that I was an authentic *carioca*—a person born in Rio de Janeiro, that is. I played an LP record with sambas so loudly that Kerstin came into the living room and begged me to lower the volume. In a fit of wrath, I shouted, "You always spoil my attempts to have fun! You sabotage my getting in touch with my Brazilian roots!" She replied that was not the case, but I ignored her and threatened to knife her if she ever meddled with my relationship with Isa, the black maid who had raised me. Alternately hollering and singing, I padded up and down the stairs, pledging everlasting love to Isa and Sonia Braga.

Though Kerstin loves to schmooze over dinner, we ate in silence. It was obvious she was frightened, and her fear pleased me, since she was now under my control. After coffee and dessert, I drove to a movie theatre and parked the car in an underground lot. Inside my head samba after samba was playing, and I sang along, cocksure that something momentous was about to happen.

Once the movie started, it became clear that I would have a hard time watching it. The characters on screen shone like icons, and I couldn't concentrate on the dialogue. Whenever Sonia Braga appeared, I thought of Isa; how she'd raised me, and one day abandoned me. Tears filled my eyes, and I felt I understood myself better. Out of the blue, an urge to be alone took hold of me. I whispered in my wife's ear that I was going to the washroom, while, in fact, I had in mind walking up and down the theatre's staircases, which I did for a while. I sang sambas and "heard" percussions and choruses performing upbeat Carnival songs. "Where have you been?" whispered Kerstin when once again I sat down next to her.

"Peeing," I said loudly, pleased that viewers all around were staring at me.

Once the movie came to an end, I told my wife I had no time to watch the credits and hurried toward the parking lot, my wife running after me. In the parking lot, I told Kerstin to wait for me by the parking lot attendant. I started the car, but instead of picking her up I drove through the barrier by the exit to the street, smashing it. I stopped the car for a few seconds and looked back, pleased that my wife and the attendant were fearfully gawking at me. I hardly remember what followed. I recall driving very fast on the Gardiner Expressway, and car after car violently swerving to their right to avoid a collision. Days later, I learned that I'd been driving fast, but in the wrong lane, against oncoming traffic.

As I drove, I became aware of red and white lights flashing ahead of me, and two policemen frantically signalling me to stop. I ignored them, but further on I noticed police cruisers parked bumper to bumper, blocking the road completely. Tires screeching, I brought my car to an abrupt halt. Several policemen surrounded me. One of them shone a flashlight on my face and ordered me to step out of the car. I was surprised at the commotion and moved my limbs slowly. Another policeman flung open the door of my car, grabbed my arm, and forced me to stand up on the road. I felt elated and sang sambas from the forties. The policemen were not amused and looked furious. As I resisted their attempts to lead me to a cruiser, they began pounding me with their fists. One of them drew a truncheon and struck me, first on the side, then on the shoulder. The more he hit, the louder I sang.

I recall standing behind iron bars, singing and demanding to see a lawyer. An hour later, a policeman told me that Harry Hardin and Peter Herschman had arrived. I was astonished, but, as it turned out, I had yelled their names and called them doctors. My friends readily convinced my jailers that I was severely ill, not high on drugs, and needed to be in a hospital.

Next, I remember sitting handcuffed in a police cruiser between my two friends, who were comforting me by saying that I was about to get treatment and would soon be all right. I dimly recall entering Toronto East General Hospital, screaming my innocence and that the police were out to drive me mad. I remember kicking hospital attendants, and my wrists and ankles were restrained to the sides of a gurney. Two men in jeans and T-shirts wheeled the gurney I was lying on through seemingly unending corridors, in and out of an elevator, then came to a stop.

“Hi, Shalom,” said a slim, thin-haired, bespectacled man in a short-sleeved, bluish shirt. “Remember me? I’m Brent Gardiner.”

Despite my frenzy, I recognized him, a psychiatrist who had, like me, been in analysis with Dr. Lesser, some ten years ago. Vaguely, I remembered us once chatting about our respective experiences in psychoanalysis, and how Brent had become an accredited analyst after years of course work and professional supervision. I had heard he was working part-time in a hospital. He must have been on call that Sunday.

Myself still tethered to the gurney, Brent bent over and whispered in my ear, evidently unwilling to be heard by the attendants, "Didn't your analysis with Dr. Lesser give you any insights?"

Despite my runaway insanity, I instantly recognized how completely inappropriate his question was. He implied that I should have known better and behaved rationally. What the hell does he want from me? I asked myself.

Despite my confusion, I faintly realized that my psychosis was somehow threatening him. I was treated by the same analyst as him, and he, evidently, was convinced that all of Dr. Lesser's patients either had been cured or at least recovered, and were not arrant madmen.

Years later, I read in the newspaper that Dr. Brent Gardiner had sexually abused a female patient and was facing disciplinary action by the college of physicians. I felt vindicated: Brent hadn't been cured and wasn't "normal" after all. Despite his high-mindedness about my madness, he had abysmally failed to maintain ethical standards. And

Brent was not the only psychoanalyst enmeshed in sexual misconduct. Another psychiatrist I was friendly with admitted to me that in the course of her analysis she sat on her analyst's lap, they kissed and fondled, but didn't "go all the way." An eminent training analyst lost his medical licence for sexually abusing a patient. Since that man had analyzed at least fifteen psychoanalysts, I told whoever listened to me that a slew of analysts were, like defective cars, in need of a recall and thorough repairs. The top rung of the ladder was rotten, I maintained, my schadenfreude entirely evident. I felt sorry for their unsuspecting patients, who had hoped their analysts would cure them and that from then on they would live happily ever after.

I, myself, though many times certifiably mad, have never violated anyone, nor breached ethical standards. No patient of mine ever needed remedial therapy because of my misconduct. And yet, despite my proper conduct, I dreaded any inquiries into my practices as calamities that would put an end to my career and my income.

The prevailing belief that a personal analysis will somehow immunize a therapist against emotional disturbances is nothing but an unfounded, self-serving, and self-congratulatory myth. Harry and Peter, both of them psychoanalysts, were shocked and pained upon hearing of patients being sexually abused by their analysts. I was initially taken aback, because the wrongdoers were in dire need of help but abysmally failed to reach out to colleagues that would have provided adequate treatment.

Admitted yet again to Toronto East General Hospital, I received standard treatment for acute mania: high doses of a major tranquilizer, plus lithium, a mood stabilizer. Within days, my speech was making sense. Friends told me that my crazed driving had made the evening news. The TV anchorman had proclaimed that Shalom Camenietzki—no title or profession mentioned—had been arrested after "erratic" driving on the Queen Elizabeth Way. Again, I dreaded my patients hearing of it and my career coming to an end. Friends, however, insisted that my problems would "blow over" by the time I returned to work. "Don't worry about being named on TV," I was repeatedly reassured. "Unlike some, you haven't fucked or fondled any patients." It took me, though, months before I calmed down enough to accept that I had acted bizarrely and dangerously.

I spent five weeks in Toronto East General. Week after week, the psychiatrist in charge said I was making slow progress and wasn't ready to resume work. When finally discharged, I found out that none of my patients had left me, although two women, who had learned that I was seriously mentally ill, soon ended their treatment with me.

One of them was a borderline woman I had been treating for two years over her turbulent relationships at work and in her personal life. She became suspicious when my wife phoned to announce that I was ill and taking a leave of absence. In a frenzy, my patient called all the hospitals in southern Ontario and quieted down only after she was told I was at the psychiatric ward of Toronto East General. When I resumed work, she stated it was scary to think that I was sicker than her, as she had never been hospitalized despite her troublesome relationships. Soon she dropped out of treatment, saying that learning about my mental illness had irreparably damaged her trust in me.

Another patient who found out the real reason for my abrupt absence from work was T., a health care professional I had been seeing for almost four years. She almost never looked at me but stared at her knees or shoes. Many times she praised me for allowing her "to hide." When I saw her after a six-week absence, she furiously chastised me for not calling her while I was ill. She wailed, "I was your baby! You held me in your arms! But for six weeks you didn't call me! You dropped me to the floor!"

She eventually found out about my bipolar disorder through a friend of hers, a psychologist at Toronto East General, who told her about my internment at her hospital. I did concede to T. that my illness had rendered me incapable of acting effectively. My admission went unanswered, since she felt illimitably entitled to be unforgiving and inconsolable. She soon found a psychoanalyst willing to treat her, and my friends congratulated me for getting rid of "a twenty-four-karat pain in the ass."

Once discharged from the hospital, I resumed seeing Dr. Mandryk. He recommended family therapy, as did the team handling my treatment at the psychiatry ward. I was referred to Dr. Garcia, an expert on family therapy. Kerstin and I saw him right after I left the hospital. Despite our pleading, our sons adamantly refused to participate in any treatment.

Dr. Garcia—a slim, bespectacled, dark-haired man with a noticeable Argentinian accent—was the only therapist I found useless in my lengthy career as madman in need of treatment. Instead of dealing with our conflicts, such as Kerstin's dread of my rages, he focused on dealing with our wayward son. True, Daniel posed many challenges, such as frequent bouts of drinking, ingrained rebelliousness, and misconduct at school. For months we discussed what to do with our son but never came to any workable solutions.

When Daniel struck up a friendship with a truant boy known to be a shoplifter, Dr. Garcia recommended we kick our son out of the house. That recommendation enraged my usually soft-spoken wife, and I thought it heartless. Kerstin and I decided to end therapy and rid ourselves of a therapist that didn't provide us with a better understanding of our troublesome son.

Chapter 8

A Decade in the Community

By 1986, Dr. Mandryk announced that he was moving his practice to Orangeville, a town about an hour's drive from Toronto. Clearly, he expected me to continue treatment at his new location, but I refused, as spending three hours a week using public transportation seemed counterproductive. Dr. Mandryk felt I should continue seeing him anyhow, since we had had a good working relationship. I, on the other hand, suspected that he was looking for work in his new location, but I was determined to help myself, not him. Eventually, he referred me to Dr. Gary Hasey, a psychiatrist at the Clarke Institute of Psychiatry, a hospital not far from downtown Toronto.

Dr. Hasey was in his early thirties when I first saw him; I was then about forty-six. As a clinician, I knew that bipolar disorder often gets worse with age, so the onset of middle age worried me. Still, I knew I needed regular treatment, especially mood stabilizers and tranquilizers, as lack of adequate drug therapy would likely result in repeated admissions to psychiatric wards.

My new psychiatrist had a thick shock of dark brown hair. His eyes were also brown and his cheekbones slightly prominent. He smiled spontaneously and inspired confidence. Already in my first session with him he declared he was no psychotherapist but was, instead, a biological psychiatrist who emphasized the medical aspects of his work. He made clear the kind of therapy he provided because I, a psychotherapist, might have certain expectations of treatment. Indeed, years later, as I complained about feeling profoundly sad and immobilized, I voiced my need to have "a shoulder to cry on." First he smiled, as if I had shared an amusing daydream, then reiterated that he was no psychotherapist, and no shoulder to cry on. So genuine was his retort that I didn't resent him; I became, instead, better cognizant of his world view and approach to therapy.

In the eleven years I was under Dr. Hasey's care, he never tried to uncover any historical reasons behind my feelings and distress. He focused in great depth on current issues, such as my work and family life. Our sessions lasted only twenty minutes, but he aptly remembered the names and circumstances of all members of my family. At times we chatted briefly about photography, as we both owned a Nikon F3 camera and were pleased with it. In his office fine portraits of his wife and young children were on display. In the first nine years of therapy with him, I saw him as my needs required. At times we would meet only every six weeks, but more frequently whenever my moods swung ominously.

I was fond of him. He never behaved as if he were out to prove that he was a warm and empathetic listener. Rather, he thoroughly examined the minutiae of my daily life, and would challenge me whenever I functioned less than optimally at home. He didn't conduct psychotherapy, but his keen interest in me as a person, a father, and a therapist was highly therapeutic. I trusted him and never held back my frequent suicidal ideas. Dr. Hasey never called me by my first name but addressed me as "Doctor Camenietzki." I always called him "doctor," as I too am never on a first-name basis with my therapists. Throughout, I avoided chumminess with them because I knew for certain that they may have to act forcefully one day, such as unequivocally telling me to enter a hospital once I became a serious danger to myself or to my wife.

And yet my relationship with Dr. Hasey wasn't formal. He insisted on paying me respect as a clinician more experienced than he was. He was quite impressed when I was appointed Fellow of the Canadian and American Group Psychotherapy Associations. It confirmed what he had probably heard through the grapevine: that I was a competent group leader who had supervised and trained dozens of neophyte group therapists.

About that time there was a disaster of sorts in France, and the French government sent a team of eleven psychiatrists to help the survivors. Dr. Hasey laughed when I asked him what he thought about psychiatrists dealing with the crisis. "What is this soccer team supposed to do there?" he asked me, wholly amused.

"Counsel the survivors," I said, astonished at his question. "There must be a lot of victims of post-traumatic stress."

"Yes," he nodded, to emphasize that he understood my position. "The psychiatrists can diagnose whatever disorders they encounter and medicate those who need it."

"What about psychotherapy?"

He laughed. "That's what I expect of you psychologists. We psychiatrists are specialists in medicine, and holding patients' hands is not our specialty. And why do the French survivors need so many psychiatrists? One or two could have done the job. I've no idea what the rest will be doing."

Dr. Hasey practised supportive, rather than exploratory, therapy, and yet he wholly subscribed to the view that medications alone were insufficient. In his eyes, sick people needed a physician's responsive listening and healing words to help them cope with conflicts and setbacks.

Dr. Hasey kept meticulous records of my moods, the medications he had prescribed, and the vicissitudes of my work and family life. Once I got into a panic about the College of Psychologists auditing my files because I was decidedly convinced that the records I kept were flawed. As is typical of me when depressed, I imagined the worst possible punishments for my presumed infractions. My psychiatrist patiently reviewed the notes I kept and found them satisfactory. To further reassure me, he told me of a colleague who had referred a patient to Dr. Hasey but had maintained no records whatsoever. Dr. Hasey felt that faulty records were the norm, and there was no need for me to dread an audit since my files were better than average.

His extensive, punctilious records became extremely important one fall, when I began complaining of unceasing melancholy moods. I wailed about my life's meaninglessness and lack of purpose and my overall feeling of going through the motions, rather than living authentically. Dr. Hasey listened intently, and then remarked that he remembered hearing similar "symptoms" before. He wanted to study my charts, to determine whether my experiences formed a discernible pattern.

Weeks later, he showed me my files—five tomes of handwritten notes. He had found a pattern in my experiences: "Every fall," he said, "you complain of not living authentically and your life lacking purpose and meaning. You become slightly optimistic by summertime. No doubt your concerns are seasonal, as are your relatively optimistic moods. People with mood disorders are sensitive to changes in season, especially at wintertime, when there's less light. Even increased dust in the air may affect some mood-disordered patients."

"Is that it?" I asked, astonished and almost offended. "Is my sense of no purpose in life just a goddamn symptom? Am I nothing but a victim of faulty brain chemistry?"

He turned grave and solemn, as if afraid of further hurting my feelings. "I don't think it's that simple. All I'm saying is that there's a seasonal component in the way some of your experiences manifest themselves."

He had unintentionally hurt my pride. I was in those days writing fiction, and preoccupations with words and phrases had made me more attuned to the significance of my own moods. Dr. Hasey's suggestion that certain experiences were reflections of my illness took away some of the singularity I attributed to my feelings. Instead, my experiences had been reduced to impersonal events devoid of uniqueness.

"Biology has triumphed over spirituality," I summed up, feeling defeated. Both creative writing and psychotherapy became, in my eyes, a dance of words ultimately choreographed by molecular events in my brain. I feared that all of my beliefs would be explained away as fanciful illusions, or as piteous symptoms of an identifiable illness.

Dr. Hasey's aversion to psychotherapy became evident on a few occasions when he failed to empathize with what I was going through. One day, he wasn't sure about the possible interactions between the various drugs I was taking. With me sitting in his office, he called the hospital's pharmacy. "Ted," he said on the phone, "this is Dr. Hasey. I have here with me a brittle patient, and I would appreciate it if you checked out any interactions among the drugs he's taking." Without glancing at my file, he listed all the medications I was taking, so knowledgeable was he of the course of treatment he had months before prescribed.

But I became upset upon hearing the adjective "brittle" being used to describe me. Yes, I had numerous times been hospitalized and taken a slew of medications, but until that moment I had never thought of myself as a fragile porcelain doll. "Brittle," however, evoked thoughts of me being a frail, sick man, and I felt so shocked that I couldn't voice my indignation at being summed up that way. That upset stayed with me for years, as I often thought of myself as a vulnerable person who must take great pains to survive an inexorable, chronic illness.

I'm entirely convinced my psychiatrist meant well. He never intended to hurt me, but his obliviousness had deleterious effects: from viewing myself as a person resolved never to capitulate, I began to consider myself as a vulnerable person afflicted with ineluctable anguishes.

Doctors are trained to avoid iatrogenic—disease-generating—questions, such as, "Do you feel dizzy when you get out of bed in the morning?" Such inquiries may induce the symptom the question is alluding to. Sick people listen anxiously to every word coming from their doctor's mouth, and a badly formulated phrase, or even a single misused word, can have iatrogenic effects. Dr. Hasey inadvertently introduced brittleness into my self-concept—the ways I think of myself. From then on, I regarded myself as a person in need of immense caution over the ways I conducted my life, since symptoms and relapses were at all times imminent.

In 1987, I stood trial for criminal negligence while operating a motor vehicle. My lawyer advised me not to plead insanity, which was truly the case, but face, instead, criminal charges, as an insanity plea might lead to indefinite detention. I had no criminal record, my lawyer reasoned, and if I voluntarily surrendered my driver's licence, the court would likely be lenient.

I felt panicky as the trial approached, fearful of serving time in jail and destroying my practice. How will I explain an extended absence to my patients? I asked myself. I decided to inform my patients I'd fallen ill, with treatment lasting as long as the duration of my sentence. Fortunately, nothing like that ever happened. I pleaded guilty to the charges and submitted references attesting to my accomplishments and good character. Prior to sentencing, the judge commented that he was impressed by my professional achievements despite my serious illness. He found me guilty and sentenced me to three months in jail, to be commuted to sixty hours of community service. My wife and I hugged each other wildly upon hearing the verdict, as we'd both expected a much worse punishment.

Before starting my community service, I spent a weekend in jail at the Mimico Detention Centre, locked up in a vast hall with dozens of detainees who milled about and smoked incessantly. The bluish-grey air stank, and I nearly choked on it, having quit smoking for six years.

After being discharged early on Monday morning, I called my wife, who met me at my office where she handed me a blue blazer, grey pants, a white shirt, and a red necktie. An hour later, I met my first patient that day. I was quite shaken, having abruptly transitioned from jailbird to professional therapist in about an hour. I wondered about the unending concealments in my life and vowed to write about them one day, feeling at once melancholy and stoical. I spent three months doing community work in a hospital for chronic patients. I spoon-fed inmates unable to feed themselves, took others out for walks outside the hospital grounds, or escorted them to the cafeteria. The work was utterly undemanding, and the only bother was having to work on weekends. Since 1985, I have not driven a car. At the time, I was terrified of driving, as I was certain I would get into a terrible accident if I ever drove again. It took me months to organize my life around public transportation, such as seeing a family doctor or a dentist close to the subway. Months later, as my mood once again swung wildly, I acknowledged that my illness rendered me unable to drive responsibly.

Once, while Kerstin was visiting her mother in Sweden, I stayed home and cared for our children. On my first Saturday without my wife around, I passed by a store and bought, on impulse, a computer, a monitor, and a printer. After practising for days, I began keyboarding and never again resorted to writing longhand, except for the handwritten notes I enter into my patients' files.

When my wife came back, she was annoyed because I had not consulted her. "I work with computers," she said. "I wouldn't buy the first thing a salesman suggested, as you did."

"I've decided to become a writer," I announced matter-of-factly.

She flinched. For decades I had been quiet about my writerly aspirations, but now I sounded determined to take up creative writing.

"What about your practice?" she asked worriedly.

"It'll be all right," I calmly replied. "I like my work as a psychologist and intend to continue it, unchanged. It's just that in my free time I'll be doing some writing."

"Is that a warning?"

"In a way, it is! I'm tired of postponing my dreams and daydreams of writing fiction. Now that I'm fifty, the time has come for me to ascertain whether or not I have any talent. Most writers start their writing careers in their teens, or at university. I'm quite behind but not discouraged."

Kerstin's eyes bespoke concern. "Have you decided to write in English, Portuguese, or Hebrew?"

"English, of course. I chose it because I speak it at work and at home. Writing fiction is always a risky enterprise, and expressing myself in my fourth language is just one of the risks I'll be taking."

"And what are you going to do about prepositions? We foreigners never know for sure whether to take up, down, in, or out—not to speak of taking on, off, or away!"

"I'll need a lot of editing, I suppose."

Like many writers, I abide by the "I don't write to be understood, I write to understand" dictum. Only after writing about my early childhood, for example, did I realize how deep my fear of abandonment by those I love really is.

Mood swings are a defining characteristic of bipolar disorder. This is easy to grasp intellectually, such as when I'm capable of reasoning and applying logic to myself. But whenever mood swings seize me, my judgment falters, even vanishes completely. Buying either photographic equipment I rarely use or expensive clothes I neither wear nor need are telling signs of pathological elations. Psychiatrists familiar with my condition waste no time and promptly ask, "Have you recently bought any shirts or cameras?"

My wife is better aware of my inchoate mood swings than I am. The latter are often signalled by my becoming inordinately argumentative—talking a lot but barely listening. And even worse are my irritability and combativeness. Kerstin once said, only half-jokingly, "I'd rather have you depressed, because you don't get furious when you're down, and it's easy to live with you. All hell breaks loose when you become hypomanic."

A peculiar feature of my manias is the fervour I experience upon reading the Tanakh, the acronym designating the Hebrew Bible. I insist on reading only the black tome that belonged to my late father. There is never a clear reason for choosing what to read, since I read feverishly whatever enters my mind: tales from Genesis or Samuel, prophesies of end of days, Psalms, or Job. Since the Tanakh is the set of books that have influenced me the most, I frequently quote from it when I become pathologically animated. I am a thoroughly secular Jew that reveres the artistry of Hebrew texts but doesn't abide by any scriptural dos and don'ts.

IN THE SPRING OF 1991, I DIDN'T SLEEP TWO NIGHTS IN a row, and yet I felt unusually alert and creative but very irascible. One evening, I returned home earlier than usual only to find our house eerily quiet. I had no idea where Kerstin and our sons were. I clambered down to the basement to work on a manuscript, but the scene I encountered enraged me: Daniel's bike was at the bottom of the staircase, and many of his bicycle tools were strewn all over the floor. "What a mess!" I hollered. I kicked the bike and his tools in a rage, and they flew in all directions. "Pest!" I yelled at Daniel. "Father killer!"

My whole life I have been a stickler for tidiness. Even at the best of times it annoyed me whenever my wife and children left things out of place. In particular, it infuriated me whenever Daniel left his or my tools outside their designated tool boxes. Over the years, I had numerous running battles with him about keeping his room in order, a futile war I lost time and again.

He was twenty-one the day he and I clashed. A rationally thinking person may have thought, "My son was repairing his bike but forgot to tidy up the basement." But instead of picking up the tools and putting them back in place, I paced the basement like a tiger raging in a cage. And the more I paced, the more enraged I became. Blinded by murderous fury, I shouted obscenities and vowed to teach my son a lesson he would never forget. I was entirely oblivious to Daniel being my son, flesh of my flesh, whose diapers I had lovingly changed and rinsed, and whose childhood I had documented in dozens of lovely photos. But I was then hypomanic and alone, and didn't have the benefit of someone pointing out how vengefully mad I had become.

I heard the door to the house opening. I rushed upstairs and saw Kerstin and Daniel enter the house with bags of groceries. Without greeting them, I ran to the kitchen and grabbed a big sharp knife. I ran toward my son, whose bags of groceries were now on the floor. "The bike! The tools!" I bellowed at him.

He looked a trifle amused, as if watching some quaint animal at the zoo.

"The bike!" I roared.

I lunged forward, grabbed his hair with my left hand, and then took the knife to the side of his neck where a few drops of blood appeared. Daniel's frightened eyes were wide open, as if he were resigned to die. Like Isaac before his father Abraham, he didn't fight back, nor did he push the knife or me aside. He just stood up, accepting that he would die young at his father's hand. I felt vindicated, even jubilant: I had, once and for all, instilled the fear of God and of his father in my perpetually rebellious son.

"Finally!" I hollered triumphantly.

"Let go of him!" Kerstin screamed as loud as she could, and I was astonished to hear her, having somehow forgotten her.

I withdrew the knife, and Daniel slowly and obediently veered his bleeding neck away from me. He straightened up, slowly walked up to the door, then sprinted down the stairs to the street. Kerstin let go of her groceries and ran after him. For hours I clambered up and down the stairs inside our home. I looked out the window every so often to see if Kerstin and Daniel were back. I placed the groceries in the fridge and in the pantry, then made myself a sandwich. In vain I tried to read, as I was still enraged, and a numbing fatigue came over me. Deep down I knew I'd committed an unforgivable crime.

I waited for my wife and son to return so I could explain myself. Lacking an audience disconcerted me and made me very anxious. By then I knew I was ill, perhaps even manic, and needed to sleep, sleep a lot, to eradicate all memories of that hideous evening. As Dr. Hasey had instructed me, I was allowed to ingest as many antipsychotic pills as necessary when mood swings assailed me. I took a heavier than usual dose of tranquilizers and went to bed.

The medications made me groggy, but I was too aroused to fall asleep. In the dark bedroom, memories of Daniel's bleeding neck haunted me. Where was that father killer? Did he go to a hospital to have his neck stitched? I expelled any remorse or guilt from my mind by telling myself that I'd taught him a lesson he had long ago deserved; his comeuppance had, at long last, arrived.

The more I thought about my difficult son, the angrier and more self-righteous I felt. My mind raced, and I gleefully anticipated confronting Daniel the next morning and further venting my rage. I rehearsed in my mind all the angry things I would fling at him, and how he'd turn speechless and fearful of me and my devastating criticisms. I was sure I would have the last word, and my fury would shut him up for good.

My alarm clock indicated it was 1:15 a.m. Despite my heavy sedation, I couldn't fall asleep. I blamed my agitated sleeplessness on Daniel the Pig and Kerstin the Softie. It bothered me to no end that she wasn't sleeping next to me. Where the hell was she?

Out of bed I rolled and checked the bedrooms. Martin, my tidy, compliant, older son was asleep in his room. Light from the living room downstairs shone. I trudged down the stairs and found Kerstin asleep on our three-seat sofa, an open book nestled in her chest. I grabbed her arm and shook her. At once she sat up.

"Why aren't you sleeping in our bed?" I furiously accused her.

She raised her palms, as if pushing me away. "I was scared." She withdrew to the very corner of the sofa. "Are you going to kill me?"

"I don't kill people!" I angrily dismissed her. "You know I love you, don't you?" She looked perplexed, my declaration of love frightening her even more. "Where is the pig?" I yelled. "Where is the brat hiding?"

"I drove him to Wellesley Hospital. On the way he was crying, poor kid."

"Crying? That's good! He's getting the message!" I sat down on the sofa.

Slowly, as if in slow motion, Kerstin got up to her feet. "We waited in the emergency, and he cried again. They stitched his neck. He's a good kid, Shalom," she said imploringly. "When the doctor asked how he got the wound, Daniel said he was climbing a fence and cut himself. He didn't say you did it. He was protecting you! And later on he told me that he didn't want to damage your reputation. It would have been terrible if word got out that you cut your own son with a knife."

Protecting *me*? I asked myself, more perplexed than worried. The idea of my professional reputation being jeopardized hadn't occurred to me. And Daniel, that awful son, was shielding me from the authorities? Despite my fury, guilt began pinching my heart. "Let's go to bed!" I raised my voice again.

Kerstin took a step back. "I'd rather sleep downstairs."

I made a fist and held it before her nose. "Don't you understand? I said we're going to bed!"

"But...I'm terrified...of you..."

"Get going! Why don't you do what I ask you to nicely? Then don't complain if I get a knife!"

Wide-eyed, she paused, then clambered up the staircase, all the while staring down at me. Her fear was palpable, and I enjoyed my capacity to intimidate her.

Once in our bedroom, Kerstin lay down with her robe on. I decided not to comment because I wanted to sleep. She read her book while I studied the ceiling fan. As sleep began approaching me, I ordered her to turn off the light, and she hurried to comply. Next morning, at work, I tried all I could to control my unbearable excitement and keep my work separate from family problems. Before lunch, I got a call from Dr. Hasey, asking me to see him in an hour. My judgment must have been quite impaired, as I didn't at all connect his call with the events of the night before. An hour later, I sat facing my psychiatrist in his office, without suspecting a thing.

"Your wife called me," Dr. Hasey said once I sat down. "She is worried about you and she—"

"No need to worry," I butted in, much louder than I'd intended. "I'm fine. I have to be back at work at 2:30."

"What happened last night?" The gap between his brows had narrowed. He looked strict and stern, and I became afraid of him.

"Just a family squabble. Had a fight with my son. Nothing serious." My face felt hot and tingly, and I knew I wasn't well.

"Your wife said you took a knife to your son's throat, and he had to be stitched up. Sounds pretty serious to me!"

"I just wanted to teach him an unforgettable lesson and frighten him, for his own good." I knew I was rambling but couldn't stop talking. And the more I talked, the hotter my face felt. Many times I told my psychiatrist that I just wanted to frighten Daniel, not harm or kill him.

"You are not well, Dr. Camenietzki," Dr. Hasey solemnly declared. "It would be better if you came to the inpatient ward for a few days. We have a free bed there."

"No way! I'm fine! Just fine! All I wanted was to scare my son. It's just a family affair! I'm not *that* ill!"

Dr. Hasey picked up the telephone receiver and said a few words I couldn't hear. "Wait here, please!" he said and hurried out of his office.

I felt trapped. What was going on? I vowed to have "a little talk" with Kerstin about calling my psychiatrist without my permission. I remembered having several appointments with patients of mine that afternoon, and I feared that my psychiatrist was taking steps to declare me dangerous to others, then lock me up in one of the hospital's wards.

I jumped to my feet and ran toward the elevator. Two tall, heavyset men in jeans and short-sleeved shirts were silently standing by the elevators' doors.

Are they waiting for me? I asked myself, knowing I couldn't fight them: over the years I'd gained weight and was no longer fit and agile. Still, I dashed to the entrance to the stairs, but one of the men ran faster than I did and blocked that door. I recall telling myself, "If you want to be back at work soon, you'd better not fight!"

"Okay! Okay!" I told the behemoths who hadn't yet said a word. In seconds I recited inside my head all I knew about the rights of the mentally ill. I felt persecuted but decided to be docile so as to be back at work as soon as possible. Somehow the orderlies silently peering at me had cleared up my thinking, and my excitement had diminished. I knew that two independent psychiatrists would examine me, to approve of what I thought of as incarceration. I vowed to speak rationally, convince the two doctors I was sane and functioning well enough to be back at work the next morning. I reiterated to myself my version of what had happened: I intended to scare my son, not harm or hurt him in any way.

"We're going to the intensive care unit on the third floor," one of the Goliaths at long last declared. He led the way, the other orderly walking behind me.

The so-called intensive care unit I was taken to consisted of a large, poorly lit room with four beds. Three men in green hospital garb lay on them. I approached the unit's nurse and said, "Could you please make sure the psychiatrists examining me will interview me now? This fucking imprisonment is costing me a small fortune! I intend to be out of this shithole this evening."

She nodded approvingly of I knew not what, but said nothing. Slowly, I strode to the unoccupied bed, lay on it, and thought of what to tell the two psychiatrists. After a while I felt restless, rolled out of bed, and walked up to the nurse. "May I have a Bible?" I asked demandingly, but as those words left my lips I regretted speaking up so forcefully. You'd better curb your tongue, I told myself. Otherwise, the nurse will report to the almighty shrinks that you're behaving inappropriately.

As the nurse stayed put, I asked her once again to hand me a Bible. "The Old Testament, in Hebrew," I couldn't help pontificating, "is the best translation of Scripture there is!" Yet again I told myself to watch out for the way I spoke, so as not to be designated "a difficult patient."

The nurse rummaged through a pile of books in a large cardboard box. "Sorry," she said apologetically, "we don't have a Bible."

"A nuthouse without a Bible," I erupted. "What's the matter with Gideons International? Do they discriminate against intensive care units?" I blurted out sarcastically, and after a pause I asked, "What will comfort me in this hour of distress?"

"We have other books in the box. Would you like to give them a try?" she said warmly, a professional helper dealing with a troublesome soul.

"No thank you!" I yelled. "If you're not in possession of the book of books, I don't want any. I'm going to take a nap."

"Good idea! Get some rest."

Right before dinner, a female psychiatrist who was about thirty years old interviewed me. I admitted to having been *slightly* hypomanic the night before and taking a knife to Daniel's throat to frighten him. I denied any intentions to harm or kill.

"Are you hypomanic now?" she pointedly asked.

"A little bit. But I'm no danger to anybody." I knew for certain that by admitting to being somewhat ill, that psychiatrist would conclude that I had good enough insight into my condition. That would work to my advantage, I said to myself, quite proud of the self-assured way I was conducting myself.

Next morning, after breakfast, another psychiatrist, this one a tall, good-looking young man, interviewed me. Yet again I played the role of a harmless, slightly disordered individual. I answered his questions only after lengthy deliberation. At about noon, the woman psychiatrist came up to my bed and announced that she and her colleague found no reasons to certify me. "The clash with your son appears to have been a family conflict," she said. "We urge you to see Dr. Hasey as soon as possible." I felt at once triumphant and vindicated, having had my way with my assessors. I was sure I could patch up my relationship with Kerstin, my sons, and my psychiatrist.

Days later, I saw Dr. Hasey. He bluntly asked if I intended to continue seeing him after he had confined me to the hospital against my will. "Doctor," I said warmly, "you acted as all good psychiatrists would. To be honest, I would have acted exactly as you did, were I in charge of a crazed, assaultive patient."

Upon my return home, Kerstin and Daniel looked terrified, and only weeks later, once my mood had evened out, did they noticeably calm down. Our dysfunctional family life went on, with Kerstin and our sons grudgingly and fearfully adapting to my mood swings. I returned to the routines of working as a psychologist on weekdays and writing fiction in late evenings and on weekends.

In all, my family paid an immense price for my grievous mental illness. In my sane moments, I have always been grateful to my wife and sons for accommodating themselves to my recurring crises. Yet I've wondered whether some masochistic traits lurked behind their loyalty to me. How else to explain their devotion in the face of recurring outbursts and abuse at home?

Spouses and children often abandon a mentally ill family member when life at home becomes unbearable. Some therapists don't hesitate to confront spouses of sick people on their tolerance of the abuse associated with serious mental illness; they imply that life will be better for the entire family if the sane spouse and children leave home. But my family continued to support and comfort me despite my furies. It soothed me to remember how, prior to falling ill, I was a loving and dedicated husband and a playful and responsible father. Kerstin and my sons, I hoped, also remembered those pre-morbid ways of mine.

And in between mood swings, when I functioned almost normally, I behaved at home as kindly as possible, so as to recapture the days and weeks I had acted benignly.

Days after I assaulted Daniel, I started to experience guilt over my conduct. And weeks later I began to understand the emotional implications of a knife-wielding father assaulting his son. I experienced it, as mentioned, as a psychotic version of Abraham's readiness to sacrifice Isaac, his son, at God's behest. That I live without monstrous guilt crippling me I attribute to the years I spent in various helpful therapies.

Though trained in psychology, I came to embrace the medical model that had guided those treating me. I viewed my on-and-off madness as symptoms of an illness, not reflections of choices I had made, or something I could have willed away. I was not held fully accountable for my behaviour while psychotic and thus incapable of realizing that a serious disorder was propelling my morbid ideas and deranged conduct. And, like many gravely depressed people, I lamented that words and phrases didn't capture the essence of my torments. Verbiage about severe depressions is like pictures of Mother Earth taken from a plane thirty thousand feet above the ground: they're nothing but blurred images that fail to reveal what our planet is all about.

In a similar vein, verbal descriptions of severe depressions are, at best, indistinct and imprecise approximations of the torments that some mood-disordered people go through. Although one may use expressions such as "I feel totally emptied out inside," those verbal accounts, however well-phrased, inform very little on what profoundly depressed people go through.

I have often asked myself, Are we madmen capable of making our wretched lives tolerable, even worth living, or is it just idle talk? Are psychotics in remission in the driver's seat, or is that nothing but a sweet illusion? And is the feeling of being sane for now nothing but piteous self-deception, perhaps even a delusion?

My reply is, I'd rather live and die with dignity, empowered by my conviction that I have, to a limited extent, chosen my own destiny, and have authored the story of my life.

While manic, I couldn't pretend I was making free choices; on those days of horror, there was no mention in therapy of guilt, shame, and accountability for my actions. I was viewed as a sick man enacting crazed behaviours no one would regard as roads I'd freely taken. And when I felt guilty over bizarre actions of mine, my therapists would soothingly exclaim, "You're being too hard on yourself! Try, instead, to correct the damage your rages have caused." The latter suggestion helped me acknowledge my *mistakes*—sins or crimes were never mentioned—so as to diminish the odds of repeating them.

And, at the risk of sounding simplistic, I will note that, no matter how crazy I acted, I was expected to pay in full any and all taxes I owed, since insanity entitles no one to free lunches! Taxes, I believe, are the genuine levellers of us Canadians: whether sane or psychotic, on April 30 we all must submit detailed income tax returns, since the taxman does not consider mental illnesses as business expenses or potential tax loopholes.

The much-maligned medical model is simplicity extraordinaire. A specialist makes methodical observations of symptoms, then produces a diagnosis calling for specific treatments. This paradigm has often been vilified, said to be too simple to encompass the complexities of human behaviour—and I wholly agree. But I have learned that there is no "psychological model" or "social work model" capable of ever supplanting medical approaches to madness and insanity. Furthermore, in a single year the medical model generates ten times more research than all of its opponents and critics have ever produced in the last one hundred years. We have yet to hear of any "anti-psychiatry" or "humanistic psychology" creating empirical research that resulted in effective and humane treatments.

As a patient treated by physicians for over forty years, I can attest that the medical model allows for empathy and understanding of off-and-on lunatics such as myself. Indeed, some physicians were more understanding than others, but I was never treated like a broken clockwork running amok. Here and there, my doctors—humans after all—may have missed the mark, and on occasion their omissions hurt me. Overall, though, I believe that the suggestions my psychiatrists made were helpful, valuable, and even curative at times.

In hindsight, most medical treatments I received aborted all of my plans to kill myself. They prevented me from irreparably despairing, and helped me maintain a sense of purpose in life. My doctors made my family life, my work as a psychologist, and my writing possible. Very likely, I would not have accomplished my few accomplishments without physicians urging me to keep fighting, at home and at work, to the day I die.

Chapter 9

Down, Mostly Down

IN THE SUMMER OF 1995, I EXPERIENCED MARKED distress. Though I was often upset and sleepless, I felt for certain I wasn't gravely ill but reacting to stresses at home. Daniel was then living with us, and my feelings about my son alternated between raw anger and excessive guilt. He was drinking heavily, and even though the label "alcoholic" frequently passed my mind, I rarely uttered it, as I feared being right and my young son meeting the criteria for worrisome addiction. He made me feel impotent, as he wouldn't consider any changes to his lifestyle.

Another troubling matter was Daniel's disorderliness. After graduating from Dalhousie University, he was looking for a suitable job and living in our basement, but his room looked as if vandals had ransacked it. As in his teenage years, his belongings were strewn across the room's floor. I experienced those messes as attempts to provoke my anger, but I failed to recognize that he was, in his own way, trying to reach out to his father. I would preach to myself, "Just ignore his provocations," but this and all other forms of self-sermonizing were of no help, and I felt I'd failed as a father. It's worth mentioning, though, that despite the ugly disorder in his room, Daniel daily shaved closely, showered, and wore clean clothes, and few people would have suspected he nightly slept in a pigsty.

We had altercations over his provocative cynicism. He viewed all of humanity as corrupt and self-serving, with no one in possession of redeeming qualities. All human activities, Daniel maintained, were scams or clever ruses, and he didn't hesitate to challenge me: "Your occupation," he once commented, "is very lucrative, but doesn't help anyone." Many times I asked whether his family also was corrupt and uncaring, and he astonished me by declaring that he implicitly trusted his mother, his brother Martin, and even me—but no one else. This trust, he said, was an exception to his view that the world was nothing but an uncompassionate and greedy jungle. He would provocatively state that he was a firebrand capitalist and fanatical atheist, primarily because of the shocking effect on some people.

I felt guilty about the incident with the knife to his throat, and whenever I wasn't angry I would blame our poor relationship on myself. My impression was that he respected his mother and me because we owned a modest house in a fine neighbourhood, his mother was a professional librarian, and the family enjoyed the benefits of my private practice. But only in passing would he acknowledge his parents' achievements. Daniel often avoided looking me in the eye, one more reason to blame myself. Often I felt irritated and impatient but tried all I could to disguise my displeasure. Attempts to suppress my anger most often failed, as I would either lash out furiously, or my bottled-up frustrations would upset me deeply. I feared the stress at home would lead me into a severe depression, a worry I shared with Peter Herschman, my close friend. He advised me to enter treatment with Dr. Elliott Markson, Peter's erstwhile psychoanalyst.

I had been living without regular psychotherapy for ten years. My visits with Dr. Hasey were a source of much support, but I felt I needed more than once-a-month sessions and a focused approach to my conflicts. I knew Dr. Markson superficially, as he had consulted with Mount Sinai Hospital while I was on staff there. Already then, he had struck me as a kind and caring psychoanalyst.

He agreed to see me right away. He was punctual and unceremoniously showed me into his consulting room. By a window was a long, brown, leather couch with a stretched-out Kleenex where patients could rest their heads. I estimated that Dr. Markson was over seventy and, therefore, unable to embark on years-long analyses.

I sat on an upholstered chair, and he asked me how he could help me. I mentioned my bipolar disorder, but added that a psychiatrist was satisfactorily treating my illness and I was looking for emotional support. I mentioned my guilt and anger toward Daniel and was soon sobbing so deeply that I began shaking and couldn't find words to describe how distraught I was. He remained calm and attentive while I poured my heart out. At the end of the session, he stated that he spent winters in Florida and wouldn't be seeing me from mid-December until Passover. "If necessary," he said, "I'll refer you to Dr. Kohl, a psychoanalyst, while I'm away."

As Peter had said, he was an excellent psychotherapist, the deepest and most empathetic healer I have ever come across, heard of, or read about. His interventions were simple and unassuming, but his eyes conveyed warmth, compassion, and caring. It was always noticeable that he listened closely and understood my suffering. I quickly became attached to him. Dr. Hasey didn't mind that I was in psychotherapy with an analyst.

The examination of my conflicts with Daniel lasted about four months. By November 1995, I became extremely depressed, and Dr. Markson's treatment then consisted of soothing my despair and my sense of having failed in all areas of my life. After my sessions with him, I felt understood for hours, occasionally for days, even though my psychic torments continued unabated. He referred to my illness as *a makkeh*—Yiddish for affliction—something over which I had no control.

Dr. Markson boasted a subtle, delicate sense of humour. He would become lighthearted with me; he would joke even when I was convinced that wit and humour were beyond me. Once, in the spring, as I was obsessing over cleaning my barbecue and making it ready for the season, I felt paralyzed and could barely take care of such a simple, mundane chore. After lamenting God alone knows how many times about my suffering over the barbecue, Dr. Markson mentioned "your attempts to *sterilize* the barbecue." Despite my suffocating sadness that day, I smiled, then laughed shyly, as if apologizing for having laughed at all.

Dr. Markson was the first therapist with whom I discussed my creative writing. I told him what I was writing about, and what it meant to me. Eventually, he read a couple of my stories, and we discussed them as literary works, not reflections of my personality or my conflicts. Dr. Markson, an avid, perspicacious, and close reader, recommended some books to me and commented on the greatness of some writers. My psychiatrist was aware of my writing, and once encouraged me by saying that bipolar disorders, unlike schizophrenia, have redeeming qualities, such as the capacity of some bipolar people to write well.

Only four months after I began treatment with Dr. Markson, my moods became dangerously low. The onset of that disturbance was very abrupt, and in a matter of days debilitating symptoms took over my life completely. In hindsight, the rapidity of my bad moods morphing into profound depressions reminded me of the waves of mania and hypomania that would seize me completely in a matter of days—even hours at times.

Initially, Dr. Hasey and I thought that my very low mood had to do with the issues discussed in psychotherapy with Dr. Markson. We soon realized, however, that we could not specify clear-cut triggers that might explain the sudden onset of my severe melancholia. Endogenous depressions are not only debilitating but also often defy verbal descriptions. Some authors have advanced the notion that profound melancholies colour—or, better said, *discolour*—one's entire world view. Only those who have done battle with severe depressions, or clinicians struggling to understand their patients' condition, are able to grasp the helplessness, despair, and suicidal thoughts that eventually coalesce into a heavy ball of lead in one's chest and guts.

Within days, I developed intense suicidal ideations. I cannot specify when, exactly, I decided that my life wasn't worth living, and that I'd better put an end to my torments. But the impulses to end my life violently troubled me so deeply that I felt as if I'd harboured them all my life. I couldn't stop thinking of death—*my* death—and over time such ruminations became second nature.

In the beginning, I intensely fantasized about taking a loaded gun to my head and pulling the trigger. Those scenarios gradually became more complex, as for hours I would obsess about acquiring a handgun and ammunition. I entertained ideas of flying down south, to buy a pistol in Texas, since my psychiatric diagnosis and criminal record precluded my legally buying a firearm in Ontario. Soon

I learned, to my chagrin, that there were some bureaucratic hurdles even in the American paradise of easy-to-acquire weapons. Storekeepers, for instance, might ask me to produce proof of residence and a driver's licence, documents I didn't have. A sense of unmitigated powerlessness soon took over, and the frustration of not obtaining a weapon worsened my overall sense of discouragement and paralysis.

It's significant that I didn't think of leaving behind a final note to my family. Did I fear I might not successfully carry out my plans? The suicidal thoughts frightened me horrendously, but, in hindsight, they resembled the passion I felt while writing fiction. Indeed, I would "write" complicated scenarios of suicide, then "edit" and "redact" them until a workable narrative emerged.

When I shared with Dr. Hasey my suicidal plans, he immediately inquired whether I owned a firearm. Upon my answering in the negative, and adding that I was taking no specific steps to acquire a gun, he seemed satisfied. Yet he offered to see me weekly, instead of monthly, which I readily accepted. He didn't ask me to elaborate on the scenarios I frequently rehearsed in my mind. He ruled out active suicidal plans and concluded that seeing me weekly would abort my suicidal ideations and put an end to planning my own death.

Dr. Markson, on the other hand, became alarmed when I described what I was obsessing about. He asked me to elaborate on my fantasies, something I found hard to do, as they were in an unceasing flux. I ended up telling him the latest version of my Shalom-kills-Shalom narrative. It astonished me that it took me only two sentences to relate it, since I experienced it as a convoluted and very lengthy story.

"I want you to promise," said a wide-eyed Dr. Markson, "that you'll call me before you take any suicidal actions."

"Sure," I said.

I liked my psychiatrist's intervention better: he'd allowed me to keep my fantasies inviolate, whereas Dr. Markson's concern struck me as exaggerated, somehow. Deep down, I had described no *active* plans to kill myself. I wasn't entirely convinced that I was capable of actually carrying out any of my vivid scenarios.

"So we have an understanding," Dr. Markson summed up, looking stern and solemn, "that you'll call me if you feel like killing yourself." It bothered me that he didn't give me his home number; my promise to stay alive until I contacted him was of benefit to the doctor but did little for a patient incessantly composing script after script of violently ending his life.

It may sound incredible, but despite my torturous obsessions with suicide I continued to do almost acceptable work with my patients. It was beneficial to take a break from my obsessions and concentrate, instead, on others' plights and predicaments.

In my view, the practice of psychotherapy calls for many attributes, the most important being the therapist's unwavering and unflinching commitment to life and reality. As for my commitment to life, I doubted whether *my* life had any value, since I toyed unceasingly with the idea of ending it. But I never doubted that others' lives were worth living. I did, moreover, envy my friends, and even my family, for going through life without mass-producing narratives of dying by suicide.

In fact, as I rehearsed methods of killing myself, I became better attuned to the wretchedness of others. I sensed my patients' shame, guilt, or longings for punishment, and surprised them when I was quick to voice an understanding of the suffering they were going through. I'd had long years of training and supervision that helped me separate my own suffering from others' psychic hurt. Luckily, I had no suicidal patients in my caseload during the months I obsessed about shooting myself. But were I to encounter such cases at work, I would have asked Harry Hardin to supervise the therapy I was doing, as he had done years before, when waves of depression began eroding my self-confidence. Weekly, for a few months, I met with Harry to examine the ongoing therapy of A., a challenging patient. With his help, I managed to negotiate the dangerous eddies of doing psychotherapy while I badly tormented myself. A. blossomed in therapy and left it feeling enthusiastic over her upcoming life in New York.

In July 1996, after months of waging all-out wars against impulses to destroy myself, I suddenly collapsed and felt incapacitated to the core. In a matter of days, the scenarios of shooting myself vanished and, instead, I began obsessing about jumping right in front of a speeding subway train. These thoughts were so all absorbing that it took Herculean efforts for me to function competently at home and at work.

Days before an appointment with Dr. Hasey, my despair was so profound that I wrote a final note to my wife and children. In a page-long letter, I explained that my agonies had become unendurable, and how I saw no hope of ever feeling better. At the end, I begged my family to forgive me once they had mourned my death. I folded the note, slid it into an envelope, and left it flat on my desk. I'd convinced myself that in a few minutes an oncoming, speeding, subway train would put an end to my suffering. So unshakable was my determination to die by suicide that it didn't even occur to me to call my doctors or my friends. I had resolved to die and waited for an opportunity to walk over to the nearest subway station.

In the meantime, I continued to treat my patients as an automaton, more or less. I asked questions, I paraphrased and expanded on what they were telling me, or said to them, "We'll explore it further, next week." I dreaded doing a lousy job and felt compelled to continue working.

At home, in the evening, I told Kerstin I was very ill but didn't mention my plans to commit suicide. My inexpressive face and deep, cavernous voice must have alarmed her, and she begged me to call Dr. Hasey. I remarked, resigned to my fate, that my psychiatrist had no time to see me right away, and I'd better wait for my appointment on Friday afternoon. I was committed to killing myself on my way to my psychiatrist's office. To get my wife off my back, I complained that I needed to sleep and slowly tottered to our bedroom. At the time, I knew I was quite psychotic, but an irrefutable logic governed all my thoughts and feelings so that dying in less than forty-eight hours felt like the incontrovertibly right thing to do.

On Thursday, I continued with my work routines. I saw a few patients in individual therapy and before going home led a therapy group. None of my patients commented on my appearance, and I heard no complaints. In my heart, I knew my work was barely acceptable, as I was encountering difficulties verbalizing even simple ideas. In a daze, I listened to my patients and wondered how my upcoming death would affect them, especially those who had been seeing me for years and were attached to me—and I to them. Though I knew I would immensely disturb them, just as I would irreparably traumatize my family, I was resolved to put an end to my agonies, regardless of the impact on others. I was supremely self-absorbed, as is true of anybody about to commit suicide. No doubt, keeping my plans unknown to others magnified my isolation from family, friends, and patients, despite my deep attachment to them.

Still, I was so intent on carrying out my plans on Friday afternoon at the latest that little else occupied my mind. My suffering justified all of my actions, and I rarely considered the consequences of killing myself. Looking back at those hours, I'm thunderstruck at my total self-centredness: How could a father, a husband, and a therapist possibly maintain such an appalling self-absorption?

On Friday morning, I cancelled all of that day's scheduled appointments, except for one, a young woman that didn't pick up her phone when I called her. She came to the meeting as bouncy as a tennis ball, and vehemently described her husband's lack of finesse and subtlety whenever he sexually approached her. As she elaborated, she began to sprawl on the loveseat she sat on, her ankles about twelve inches apart from one another and the gap between them slowly growing. It was, I said to myself, an unconscious invitation of sorts for me to participate in a game of seduction. But I felt too vulnerable to challenge the provocative, nonverbal messages she was sending me. I feared upsetting her and dreaded her pleading lamb-like innocence and casting me in the role of cold, insensitive wolf. Feeling incapacitated and helpless, I let her drone on and on about her condescending feelings for her husband. I hated myself for not reacting competently, my decision to kill myself an excuse for my inadequacy and dereliction of duty.

Right after she left the room, I wrote a note in her chart—some ingrained habits are hard to bypass, even when you're about to die. I cleared my desk and placed my final note in a conspicuous place. I hoped it'd be immediately noticed when my wife and children reopened my office after the shivah, the initial seven days of mourning. Before leaving my office, I took my black leather briefcase containing a promising draft of a story, a couple of books, and two patients' charts in need of updates. I slowly walked toward the nearest subway station. My fare paid, I rushed down the stairs toward the platform of trains travelling south—toward Dr. Hasey's office, as I realized only later. Heart thumping, I stood by the northern end of the platform, so that I would hop right in front of the oncoming, still speeding train. An instantaneous, painless death awaited me, I thought.

I stared at the tunnel from which the train would emerge. Panicky and yet dying to put an end to my torments, I saw a faraway yellow light, dimly illuminating snatches of the tunnel's walls. I took a step forward. It occurred to me that there was no need to destroy my leather briefcase, so I set it down by my feet on the ground. Now I saw clearly the approaching train's two golden lights, even glimpsed the driver's cap and face. An icy wave washed over me, and I asked myself why I was weeping. "In a second I'll jump," I muttered, to summon courage and kill my doubts.

Moments later, I was staring at the row of well-lit subway cars that had come to a full stop. The doors to the cars clattered open, some passengers coming out, others entering. A few people on their way to the exit brushed against me unintentionally. A reedy beep sounded, the doors closed, and the train began inching forward. In a moment I watched the train's last car, so similar to the one in front but with no piercing yellow lights to illuminate the tunnel. Patiently, I waited for the next train, my resolve still strong. My briefcase stood on the platform looking like a dejected orphan, so I picked it up and felt better keeping my right hand occupied, the other one stuffed into a pocket. Soon I recognized the wide swath of light of an approaching train, and yet again I placed the briefcase on the platform by my foot. This time, I vowed, my dread of dying wouldn't stop me. Inexplicably, my final note flat on my desk crossed my mind, and I egged myself on: "Be a man!" I glanced at the train's two yellow lights and its driver's blurred image. Why was he smiling?

I came to when a passenger lightly smacked my shoulder on his way into the car before me. "Why didn't you jump?" I murmured accusingly. "Coward! What do you have to lose? A quick death is nobler than a long, intolerable life!" I vowed to jump right in front of the next train, but fears of a harrowing, prolonged death took over. I imagined my skin being ripped like newsprint and my knees and shins crushed like wooden matches. What about my eyes? I asked myself, as I noticed an elderly woman staring at me.

The next train lit the tunnel and fast approached the station. This time I noticed my face being cooled by the wind generated by the speeding train. "Still alive, eh?" I taunted myself. "How lily-livered can you get?"

My mouth full of saliva, I glanced at my watch: over an hour till my appointment with Dr. Hasey. To cope with the pressure to kill myself, in a flash I climbed up the stairs to the station's exit. Once on Yonge Street, I hailed a cab and told the driver to take me to the Clarke Institute.

To kill time, I took a walk around the Clarke building but felt so weak that I soon entered the hospital. Heart beating wildly, for a whole hour I sat in Dr. Hasey's waiting room. Head emptied out of any thoughts, I stared at the art work on the walls. Patient after patient entered my psychiatrist's office and left about twenty minutes later.

"I noticed you came very early today," commented Dr. Hasey once I perched on a chair inside his office.

"I cancelled almost all my appointments today." My tremulous voice came as a surprise to me.

He leaned back on his swivel chair, raised his chin, and peered at me intensely. "Dr. Camenietzki, you've never cancelled any appointments! Even with a high fever, you do your work. What's up?"

I eagerly replied, "I stood on the subway platform but couldn't jump in front of the fast-approaching train."

Looking strict and stern, he examined me. "It was the healthy you that decided not to kill yourself." His forefinger wiped his lower lip and chin, then he uttered, "We've an opening on our ward. It'd be better if you came in for a few days, to get over the hump. You've been ill for a long while, and time has come for inpatient treatment."

I felt relieved. His "come in for a few days" made me feel understood. I looked forward to a locked ward, away from subway trains, musty platforms, and dark tunnels. I wanted, above all, to feel safe and protected. "My wife will pick me up at 4:30. I'll ask her what she thinks."

With an outstretched hand, he signalled me to stop. "It's all right, Dr. Camenietzki. I'll talk to her when she comes. Meanwhile, I'll call the nurse, and she'll escort you to your room."

He stood up. "Right now," he said, "we have to keep your health in mind. Please take your briefcase with you, and I'll show you the nurses' station."

The ward was eerily quiet when I entered. No one was pacing the corridors, as I'd expected. As it later turned out, most inpatients were on weekend passes and had been instructed to socialize with family and friends. Spending the weekend cooped up on the ward was against the unit's policy.

On Monday morning I told Marilyn, the tall, slim nurse I'd been assigned to, that I had incessant thoughts of running to the nearest subway station and killing myself. "This time," I declared, "I intend to succeed."

She was then counting pills, placing them in tiny white paper cups, then doling out morning medications to her patients. She stopped and, eyeing me sternly, said, "What about your family? How would *they* feel if you killed yourself? What sort of message would you be giving your sons about the value of life?"

I was furious: not only had she failed to understand my plight, but she also confronted me harshly.

Instead of replying, I held the cup with my pills and turned around. I was too vulnerable to express indignation at Marilyn pelting me with the consequences of suicide.

Minutes later, I met with Dr. Hasey. I complained about Marilyn's insensitivity, but he eyed me gravely, a surgeon about to amputate a gangrened leg. "You're in an inpatient unit," he said. "Any suicidal gesture demoralizes the staff and immensely disturbs patients on the ward. You *must* face the harm your suicide will do to your family, friends, and patients. You're angry because Marilyn reminded you of your responsibilities. Yes, you are ill and fragile, but you're still accountable! But—" he paused, "—you look perturbed, doctor!"

"I feel misunderstood and lonely. I can't share with the staff how I really feel."

He lifted himself up from his chair. "Here on the unit we'll support you, provided you make no attempts to kill yourself," he said while escorting me to the door. I knew he had other patients waiting to see him that morning, and yet I resented him cutting our meeting short.

Two days later Marilyn astonished me by advising me that "the team" had given me a pass to leave the ward for half an hour, unescorted. I still felt frail and scared of leaving the ward, my safe womb, but she reassured me that all

I was expected to do was to take a brief walk on College Street, just outside the hospital. Fearful, I left the ward and began pacing outdoors slowly, the daylight blinding me. I felt woozy, so I walked around the block, afraid of the cars and trucks trundling the street. A streetcar clattered by, and in a panic I rushed back to the ward, like a frightened toddler rushing to grab his mother's skirt. I reported my fears to Marilyn, and she praised my courage and determination. I felt I was a fool, dreading the street traffic as if I were facing a firing squad.

From that afternoon on, I went on longer and longer unescorted walks outdoors. On the ward I noticed some six patients, always the same ones, congregating and chatting. I joined the conversations and spoke about Dr. Hasey, the medications I was taking, and their side effects. Soon we began revealing more personal information, such as our lives prior to entering the hospital. As I look back, I feel I derived no less help from these spontaneous, leaderless group sessions than from any therapies available on the ward.

Months after my discharge from the hospital, I discussed those spontaneous meetings with colleagues who, like me, specialized in group psychotherapy. Most of them expressed amazement at fragile inpatients taking therapeutic initiatives on their own. Only one psychiatrist with much experience with inpatient treatments was acquainted with patients taking the initiative and meeting in leaderless groups.

One afternoon, on my third week on the ward, I felt like a minor storm was brewing inside me. I was playing Ping-Pong with more zest than usual, even kidded with one of the nurses in the room. And yet I felt as dejected and troubled as I had been for months. Next morning, when I discussed the previous afternoon with Dr. Hasey, he smiled. "First the patient looks better, and only then he feels better!" he said. What his oracular saying meant was that Paxil, the medication I was taking, was kicking in. I *looked* better, as my lively behaviour in the Ping-Pong room showed, though I didn't feel better yet.

This led to my discharge the following Friday, as hospitalizations were deemed expensive. Patients were discharged at the first sign of change in themselves, or in their therapists' assessment.

Upon discharge from the Clarke, I resumed work at my office. My mood was markedly high, and my psychiatrist didn't hesitate to announce that I was hypomanic on account of the Paxil I was taking. Consequently, he decreased the dosage I was on, but my elevated mood persisted. At home, I was cantankerous and combative; minor things angered me, and I became loud and verbally abusive whenever I didn't have my way. Later, as my mood improved, Kerstin began to imitate my abusive speech: "My way or the highway!" she hollered, then mimicked my bellowing, "What I say goes!" And whenever she broached family problems I would, according to her, fire off a standard excuse: "I've more important things to do!"

After each bout of hypomania, I crashed and experienced moderate, but still distressing, depressive moods. Dr. Hasey commented that hypomania was like borrowing money from a loan shark: "You end up paying a heavy price for the short-lived good feelings you borrowed."

While hypomanic, I began writing a novel about a paranoid schizophrenic writer who was locked up for twenty-eight years at Nine Ninety-Nine, the slangy name for the psychiatric hospital near downtown Toronto. I wrote that book in a frantic pace, sitting at the computer for long hours. That I somehow managed with so little sleep was in itself a symptom of a disorder. Most chapters of the novel described a treatment the mad narrator received but found either useless or damaging. I elaborated on the social and political implications of the therapies that madman received. The writing was peculiarly polemic; a reflection of my elevated mood and the protagonist's disordered thinking.

A year after my first hospitalization at the Clarke, a debilitating depression struck me, and again I engaged in intense, obsessive plans of jumping in front of a speeding subway train. Dr. Hasey was on vacation at the time, so I went to the emergency department at the Clarke, where I was instructed to come back after the weekend to be reassessed. I wanted to be admitted because I hoped that spending time on the ward would be as helpful as it had been a year before.

Days later, once the admitting psychiatrist established that I was dangerously suicidal, I returned to the mood disorders ward. That hospitalization was atrocious, as my psychiatrist was away and the psychiatrist in charge interviewed me briefly and only once. I found no new group of patients to talk to, and the nurse assigned to me was so unempathetic that I called her clueless to her face. It was, in short, a waste of my time to walk the ward's corridors up and down and wait for medications to kick in. After two weeks, I asked to be discharged, and went back home still very depressed but free of impulses to kill myself.

When Dr. Hasey resumed work, he announced that he had taken a position in an outpatient clinic in Hamilton, Ontario, where he would be spending time doing research. I knew of his interest in research and wished him well. I'd seen him for ten years but had never become deeply attached to him, in part because Dr. Hasey systematically maintained distance, such as never addressing me by my first name. Before leaving, he phoned Dr. Sagar Parikh and, in my presence, introduced me as a "compliant, psychologically minded, and well-motivated patient." By then I'd become used to Dr. Hasey discussing my illness over the phone while I was present in his office, so I didn't particularly mind that phone call.

On my next visit, Dr. Hasey announced that Dr. Parikh would be my new therapist. I didn't feel particularly sad saying goodbye to Dr. Hasey, but I was grateful for his attentiveness over the years. His attitude was strictly professional, ethical, and correct, but lacked compassionate warmth. His somewhat arid demeanour would not have encouraged people to pay out of pocket for long-term therapy with him. He went on to become a researcher in the area of magnetic brain stimulation and acquired a good reputation.

Despite mood swings and hospitalizations, my writing blossomed. Researchers have shown there is a small correlation between literary talent and madness; excelling in writing poetry, for example, correlates with the presence of mood disorder in the writer himself, or in his blood relatives.

By the late nineties, ten of my stories had been published in literary magazines, three of them in the eminent *Dalhousie Review*—not a bad track record for a part-time author with very little education in literature. At one point I even considered closing my practice and becoming a full-time author. But I gave up on that plan upon recalling my immense worries over my career as a psychologist coming to an end whenever I became gravely ill. After lengthy deliberation, I decided that the psychologist in me was at the core of my identity, something I wasn't prepared to give up. I loved the practice of psychotherapy, especially the stimulating, intimate, and helpful dialogues with people emotionally attached to me, and myself reciprocating their involvement. I came to the conclusion that were I to close my office, I'd especially miss the gratification inherent in leading therapy groups, the most stimulating and exciting aspect of my work. By way of compromise, I began defining myself as "half-time psychologist, half-time author." I was about fifty-eight at the time and had no plans to retire anytime soon.

In 1998, I began seeing Dr. Parikh regularly. As stated, I have no interest in my therapists' private lives; still, I knew that he had done his undergraduate studies in the United States because of the degree hanging on a wall in his office. It was quite obvious from his soft accent that he was either from India or Pakistan. He is slightly swarthy, and his skin colour posed initial concerns. As a young child, a black woman raised me, and to this day I still associate dark skin with figures pampering and caring for me. Dr. Hasey's comment that Dr. Parikh had been a resident he had supervised, and a trainee who became a fine clinician, helped me get over my ambivalence over intimate contacts with a non-Caucasian.

Dr. Parikh is of average height, wears eyeglasses, and is quite bald except for a garland of short black hair about his temples. His gaze is keen and focussed, and he is a sharp dresser. Initially, I was unsure about the poor eye contact he maintained with me. He would, as I poured my heart out to him, gaze at his shoes or at the floor, as if preoccupied with their condition. I commented that his staring at the floor disturbed me; he took my complaints to heart, and he began keeping better eye contact.*

* Early in 2015, when Dr. Parikh was about to leave Canada for a position in Michigan, he shared with me that when he first met me he was a resident, not a full-fledged psychiatrist. He...

As a psychiatrist, Dr. Parikh proved more daring and less fearful of my mood swings than previous doctors: even though he knew that my taking Paxil might make me manic, he prescribed heavy doses of that drug when my moods became alarmingly low. He tried a variety of antidepressants on me, finally settling on a cocktail of those drugs with a mood stabilizer. He trusted that if my moods got out of hand, I'd be able to medicate myself and take the right amount of tranquilizers. His trust helped create a good rapport between us.

Usually, Dr. Parikh was less directive than other psychiatrists. He rarely told me which medication to take. Rather, he spoke as if he were a consultant in psychopharmacology who shared with me technical information but let me choose the drugs I'd take. In that way, I felt I was a partner in managing the handful of pills I daily ingested. But whenever Dr. Parikh needed to intervene, such as when my judgment was faltering, he would unambiguously state his opinions and recommendations.

...admitted feeling slightly intimidated then, because he was a trainee treating "a distinguished psychologist." That surprised me, as he had never before disclosed anything personal about himself, and I felt slightly embarrassed since I never know where I ought to place my hands whenever people pay me compliments. At work, I am at ease with words of gratitude, which are frequent in the course of therapy, and I have become accustomed to them. On the other hand, I rarely lose composure whenever patients inveigh against my style or my personality.

He was much concerned about my relationship with my sons. He often asked me about them, and his good memory for details sometimes astonished me. I soon learned that he was very interested in psychological approaches to bipolar disorders. He himself subscribed to the cognitive behavioural approach to psychotherapy and its emphasis on correcting distorted thoughts and beliefs. Though he didn't object to my seeing an analyst like Dr. Markson, he suggested I be practical: instead of sessions with a quasi-retired analyst who spent winters in Florida, he recommended treatment with a younger analyst available eleven out of twelve months. That bit of advice suggested to me that Dr. Parikh's insight into the subtleties and strengths of one's relationship with a therapist may have been limited, and at times I wondered whether he truly understood my attachment to him. Though he believed in the efficacy of the cognitive behavioural model, he said he had no time for treating me once a week, as my condition required. He did, however, recommend a psychiatrist, who in turn referred me to Dr. Natasha Graham, a family physician specializing in cognitive therapy, and in bipolar disorders in particular. As if to counter my fears of family doctors practising psychotherapy—I had once written a biting satire on that topic—Dr. Parikh added that Dr. Graham was an expert who trained physicians in the use of cognitive therapy.

My dread of running out of money prevented me from seeking therapy from a psychologist—which I preferred but didn't pursue—since I would have to pay out of pocket for my treatment. I opted to go into treatment with a physician covered by the Ontario Health Insurance Plan, though in truth I could afford private treatment.

My problems with money continued, as I either spent too much or hoarded it senselessly. One year, I was so convinced that I'd have no money to pay the year-end income tax instalment that I saved as much as possible. When time to pay taxes came, I found I had saved over twenty thousand dollars, more than twice what I owed. And yet, weeks later, I began worrying moderately about next year's tax instalments.

Dr. Graham's office was on the forty-ninth floor of a downtown high-rise. I stepped out of the elevator into a large and pleasantly furnished waiting room. A well-dressed receptionist oversaw the ins and outs of the place from behind a large desk. I'm always ten minutes early for all my appointments, so I was told by the pleasantly smiling receptionist to take a seat and wait. I was quite anxious because Dr. Graham would be the *third* therapist I was seeing concomitantly! In the province of Ontario, the practice of psychotherapy by physicians is covered by public health funds, and at times abuses happen. Dr. Markson not only didn't object to my seeing a second psychotherapist but even encouraged me to do so. Caught in a web of therapists and treatments, I saw myself as a vulnerable person in need of great amounts of therapy to survive.

Perhaps, I asked myself, was all the fuss about my treatment due to my being a therapist myself? I was, after all, in charge of a few dozen patients, some of them very dysfunctional, and a few of them severely depressed and potentially suicidal. My continued capacity to function as a therapist was in the public good, I reasoned. An inner voice, however, protested that there was nothing special about myself. Your therapists, I told myself, are doing what they would have done for any other sick man. Don't flatter yourself!

When I met Dr. Graham, I was sixty-one years old, and she looked twenty years younger than me. She was attractive; her large hazel eyes looked at me softly, and her hair was brown, undulate, and silky. She spoke calmly, and her bedside manner bespoke kindness and patience.

After a few assessment interviews, she introduced me to her approach to cognitive therapy. She spoke little about "negative thoughts" or "core beliefs" and conducted our sessions as most psychotherapists would. We discussed my symptoms at length, and she expressed sympathy. She did, however, administer the Beck Depression Inventory once a month early in our work, and urged me to do the "homework" she assigned every week. The "homework" usually involved keeping a journal of my symptoms, or recording the work I did around the house, something I dreaded in those days.

Throughout the eight years I was under Dr. Graham's care, the therapy focussed on my intense feelings of helplessness every time my moods dipped. Subjectively, I felt that whenever I had a task to perform, such as washing dishes, I would "hear" voices inside me declaring, "Can't do it! Can't do it!" Such experiences of invalidism made me flinch at the mere thought of carrying out even small tasks, such as changing a light bulb. That I endlessly obsessed about each step I ought to take was an immense problem, since the more I analyzed what needed to be done, the more disempowered and immobilized I felt.

Though I'm no procrastinator when healthy, feelings of helplessness drove me to postpone chores only I could do, such as maintaining files at the office. The thought of filling out a form, for example, appeared insurmountable. I would castigate myself, such as calling myself a lazybones that ought to feel ashamed of his unmanly passivity. I felt guilty over Kerstin doing virtually all necessary chores, including work traditionally regarded as "a man's job." I ceaselessly called myself uxorious and a burden on my wife.

To Kerstin's credit, she rarely complained, as she remembered me being active around the house for many years; every spring, for instance, I energetically tidied up and cleaned the garage, basement, and back and front yards. Without ever being reminded, I nightly cleaned the kitchen so thoroughly that it seemed as if cardiac surgery was about to be performed there. Many times my wife commented that my condition was noticeable, what with my hands buried deep inside my pockets, and my face looking like I was wearing a mask of confusion and fear.

Dr. Graham's approach to my recurring experiences of being helpless was persistent and consistent. She was predictably kind and nonconfrontational, though she instructed me to continue with work at home and in the office. Procrastinating made my condition even worse, she frequently reminded me. She shared with me simple, common sense ideas, such as breaking down difficult tasks into small components, working on one component and then the next. Still, while incapacitated I found it reassuring to hear her recite such commonplaces. In my eyes, the homilies she declaimed were indisputable, verifiable truths. Her patience with me was inexhaustible. Once we spent twenty-five minutes reviewing the steps I ought to take in order to repair a bookshelf at home. We planned it painstakingly, as if we were generals coordinating an offensive by infantry and tank divisions, backed by heavy artillery and hundreds of fighter bombers. She was so meticulous and encouraging that I temporarily overcame my dread and managed to repair the bookshelf surprisingly well.

In every session Dr. Graham repeated the lessons from the previous week. At home or at the office, I would recall her voice whenever I fought against my urges to give up. I slowly internalized her unflinching belief that I could overcome my passivity and defeatism.

Countless times Dr. Graham challenged me with, "You may *feel* helpless, but you're not helpless!" Also helpful was her notion that "Feelings are not facts!" My feelings of being a failure in all areas of my life, for example, were said to be feelings and beliefs with no factual evidence to back them up. Tactfully, she frequently emphasized that, despite my debilitating symptoms, I was still earning a six-figure income a year, a collection of my stories had been published, and my colleagues regarded me as an expert on group therapy. She readily empathized with my suffering but countless times observed that I was making progress, even getting better. At times I doubted whether my so-called improvements were as real as she portrayed. But when I look back on the years she and I struggled to improve my life, I must admit that I gradually felt less and less disabled, and my delusions of poverty significantly receded.

In my therapy with Dr. Graham, I was at times so attached to her that I looked upon every session as an oasis surrounded by worries, disgust, and despair. Though I have no patience with "positive thinking" of any stripe or colour, I would come fifteen minutes early to our weekly sessions, craving her exhortations to solve my problems rationally.

Her approach to therapy was radically different from the way I practised. I believed in exploring deep-seated feelings, acquiring insights, and rearranging one's life accordingly. Dr. Graham emphasized that strategies for overcoming disturbances must be rooted in pragmatic logic. Despite the disconnect between the way I worked with my patients and how Dr. Graham treated me, I chose to ignore it, since I felt I was improving slowly but noticeably. I admired her and felt grateful for all the help she extended.

Dr. Graham always appeared relaxed and confident. At times she offered me coffee, which we sipped while talking. Once she felt hungry, apparently, and munched on a bagel. I enjoyed her spontaneity and her ignoring the dictates on how therapists "should" behave in the presence of their charges. At times she even took phone calls during my sessions. I didn't mind such unorthodox practices, since her spontaneity and utter absence of self-consciousness were at once amusing and appealing.

Once, after she stopped assigning me "homework" and we spent time discussing my daily conflicts, she laughed as she remarked, "I offer meat-and-potatoes therapy, not gourmet dishes." Indeed, her down-to-earth approach to life's problems often felt like a cool breeze on a hot and muggy summer day. And yet the few times I brought up long-term issues, such as my idealizing the maid who had mothered me, she offered keen, sophisticated observations on how I was conducting my life and coping with my emotions.

My treatment with her convinced me that warmth and empathy in therapy are not at all consequences of the theories therapists swear by but expressions of their personality and style. I found it comforting and reassuring that Dr. Graham not only was well-read on professional matters—she knew by heart all the minuscule ins and outs of bipolar disorder—but also read novels whose characters absorbed her for weeks.

About a year and a half into my treatment with Dr. Graham, I stopped seeing Dr. Markson. In part it was due to him having little time to see me regularly, as he was winding down his practice. Also, I felt our work had reached a natural end. Dr. Graham, the most helpful of all my therapists, taught me survival strategies and techniques to overcome despair and helplessness. I no longer craved Dr. Markson's empathetic comments, since they made me feel good for hours, occasionally for a couple of days, but didn't equip me with tools to surmount my godawful moods and relapses. I parted with him very amicably, and, years later, when a collection of my stories was published, I mailed him a copy of the book, since it was important, in my eyes, that he read portions of it. He had encouraged my writing but avoided shallow interpretations, such as a presumed correspondence between my personal life and the fiction I was writing.

As with almost all forms of depression, I had notable problems concentrating. Reading newspapers and magazines was possible, but as I attempted to read fiction, I would lose track of what I'd read after a couple of paragraphs. My mind wandered, and I felt confused and frustrated, as the artistry of great writers wasn't improving my own writing. I felt discouraged and impotent but didn't give up; instead, I took steps to improve my condition.

First, I reread short stories. The familiarity with plot, characters, and structure of those fictions allowed me to focus better, and I experienced some pleasure in revisiting those works. The second step was less straightforward: as I dreaded my writing becoming dull and uninspiring, I would write down words whose meaning I either didn't know or felt unsure about their usage. Collecting words and phrases unknown to me bolstered my confidence, and kept me alert and capable of writing creatively despite my flawed concentration. With time, my writing improved and my self-confidence grew, having resolved a thorny issue without help from my healers.

While distraught or insecure, I would encourage myself by muttering my writerly mantra: "The only way to write is well, all locutions chosen for their clock-like precision, and ideas expressed in ten words or less." Doggedly giving myself pep talks kept me more alert and more focused than what I had initially deemed possible.

While severely depressed, I suffered a great deal on weekends. To begin with, it's not easy for a hard-working person such as myself to spend two whole days doing no stimulating professional work. Often I felt like time had ground to a permanent halt, and there would be no end to my distress. Eyes closed, I would sit on a sofa, feel terribly sorry for myself, and yet take few constructive steps. Kerstin felt bad about my condition and would offer cups of tea to distract me away from my morass. To help me fight my despair and inactivity, she'd suggest we go for a stroll, visit a museum, or watch a movie.

Solutions evolved slowly out of Kerstin's desire to convert to Judaism for the second time. Her first conversion was a lightweight affair: a Reform rabbi, while we lived in the States, assigned her a list of readings and met with her for a few conversations. He didn't even mention her immersing in a *mikveh*, a ritual bath, as a more traditional rabbi would have required. This time she spoke with a

Conservative rabbi, who demanded that Kerstin and I take a year-long course on Judaism, with the *mikveh* a non-negotiable requirement. To Kerstin's astonishment, I agreed to attend the studies, as it was obvious the conversion was very important to her. She explained the urge to convert as a lifelong need to connect with God and a community of believers; she'd been brought up in a secular home in largely irreligious Sweden, where all her life she had found no outlet for her religious yearnings. Our son Daniel told me that the timing of the conversion had to do with his mother's aging and her nest becoming empty, now that he and his brother were living on their own.

Part and parcel of Kerstin's second conversion involved attending shul on Saturday mornings. I was quite receptive to that idea, as I thought it would be a year-long duty, no more. In that year I learned to sing hymns, and my good command of Hebrew helped me navigate the Siddur, the prayer book. Kerstin was grateful for my attending services, and the conversion process brought us closer.

In the fall of 2000, I again experienced a disabling depression. Unlike previous bouts, the weekends were more manageable this time around, as I was busy attending shul on Saturdays. At times we had lunch at the home of Rabbi Tennenbaum, Kerstin's sponsor. Quite often we attended events on Friday nights or on Saturday afternoons, and at times we were busy even on Sundays.

Judaism is a way of life, I learned in the conversion course. Each weekend it occupied us for many hours; I attended many events and programs and felt better, having a structure imposed on my otherwise immensely abject weekends. I willingly prayed to a God I didn't believe in, rather than wallow in bleak despair. "In the wars I wage against severe depressions," I encouraged myself, "any and all weapons are *glatt kosher*"—entirely pure, entirely acceptable.

I've a reasonably good voice, and Kerstin and the community appreciated the way I sang the hymns and prayers. Thus, serious mental illness drove a lifelong irreligious Jew into becoming a shul-goer. I enjoyed reading prayers and weekly marvelled at the beauty and power of Hebrew poetry. Though I found the notion of God creating heaven and earth in six days and resting on the seventh preposterous, the shul's ambience and the kind people I met weekly enhanced my understanding of religious practices.

In 2001, Kerstin and I joined the Narayever congregation in downtown Toronto, a traditional but egalitarian community. I liked most of the congregants, though none of our new friends at the shul knew of my disorder. They would, no doubt, be amazed to find out that I remained, at bottom, an atheist who would rather sing hymns and prayers than succumb to crippling symptoms. At the time, I comforted myself by saying that attending religious services stemmed from a need to belong. Given my thorough Jewish upbringing, it never crossed my mind to belong to the Swedish Lutheran church, say, or to a political party.

Based on my experience as a patient and psychologist, I concluded that the drive to continue living my often wretched life was nothing but a biological imperative. Even psychotics wish to continue living, even while confined to sterile wards that diminish one's sense of dignity. Like all suicidal people, I wanted those I would leave behind to believe that the decision to take my own life had come only after exhaustive thinking.

But whenever suicidal ideations are not in control of my life, I affirm that there's nothing thoughtful or rational about suicide; it is, rather, driven by despair over one's incapacity to mitigate physical or emotional suffering. Survivors of suicidal attempts know that toying with death is impulsive and irrational, at times even shallow. Once they think clearly, they eventually recognize that "succeeding" at suicide would have left beloved ones traumatized for life. The notion that people don't commit suicide out of cowardice is utter nonsense; bravery is what keeps disturbed people from hanging themselves, overdosing, or blowing their brains out. The self-preservation instinct, the most powerful of all instincts, is what allows us to navigate the stormy oceans of psychic torments, self-hatred, and immobilizing despair.

Psychotherapy with suicidal people is one of the most difficult tasks there is. The therapist must show unwavering and unflinching belief in the value of life, without ever minimizing the distress that drives some people to regard suicide as the only way out of their affliction. Striking a therapeutic balance between compassion and unyielding belief in life's worth is difficult to attain.

Once, while I was hospitalized at the Clarke Institute, Dr. Hasey asked me "not to talk too much" about plans to kill myself with the nursing staff. I could hardly believe my ears and, despite my paralyzing despair, asserted: "If I can't discuss my plans for suicide, what the hell am I doing here? I'm pretty sure that a lot of bartenders would listen to me from the first to last word!"

Dr. Hasey calmly remarked that, a couple of days before, a hospitalized young man had hanged himself in his room. Hence, the nursing staff was shaky and demoralized, the reason why I had been asked to abide by an unheard-of request. The moral of this vignette is that a few severely suicidal patients will kill themselves no matter where you confine them. No hospital, jail, or straitjacket will ever stop someone implacably determined to put an end to his or her torments. Such difficult cases, however, are a small minority among those contemplating suicide.

My worst depression ever began in April 2001. Like the majority of my mood swings, within days my life became unendurable. Though I'm convinced that neither written nor spoken words do justice to the torments a severely depressed person goes through, I'll briefly outline my affliction. By mid-April, I felt devastated by indefinable distress and as frail as if I were one hundred years old. In particular, it troubled me greatly that my thinking had slowed down, and I often was unable to affix words even to mundane experiences such as fatigue or thirst. Yet again impulses to sneak out of the house, rush to the nearest subway station, and jump in front of a speeding subway train hurtfully affected all my thoughts and feelings.

Drs. Parikh and Markson saw me as much as their schedules permitted, but I experienced no relief. I was convinced that whatever lessons previous treatments had taught me had completely vanished. So intense were my suicidal plans that I resigned myself to the idea that I would soon kill myself. I remember staring at my wife and sons, very saddened by the prospect of saying a final goodbye to them.

On April 15, a Sunday, I felt so driven to commit suicide while having lunch that I begged Kerstin to drive me to the Clarke Institute immediately. For hours I waited to be seen by the resident on call, but instead Peter Herschman, my good friend, came to visit me. For years he had been urging me to call him, day or night, if I felt desperate. "I'll take you to a hospital," he had promised more than once. And yet his visit to the Clarke embarrassed me, since I had ignored his generous offer and, moreover, couldn't put into words feelings of gratitude now that my thinking had frightfully slowed down.

The resident who examined me—a slim, brown-haired woman in her twenties, who spoke English with an Indian accent—grew alarmed as I talked to her and didn't hide her feelings. I must have looked very ill as I haltingly rambled on about "self-murder." It took her just a few moments to decide to hospitalize me. "You're very unwell," she said, "and I'm looking for a hospital bed other than here in the

Clarke, because ours are all taken." She left the examining room for a short while and soon returned to announce that a bed was available at Mount Sinai Hospital. Despite my numbness, I managed to whisper, "I was...there..."

She furrowed her brow and pursed her lips. "Where? At the Mount Sinai? When?"

"I was...on staff...there...long time ago..."

She tilted her head to hear me better. "Are you a doctor?" She glanced at her notes to make sure she understood me.

"Psychologist." I was relieved to find a word that partially defined my identity.

"I see." She straightened up. "Are you embarrassed to go into the Mount Sinai?"

I remained silent. Despite the hollowness inside me, the phrase "feeling awful" occurred to me, but I couldn't utter it.

"I can get you a bed in Stoufville," she said, her piercing eyes now boring holes into mine. "Is that okay?"

I thought at length and recalled how Stoufville was a long drive north of Toronto. Too hard for family and friends to visit me—I'd be forgotten. "That's all right," I mumbled, "I'll go into the Mount Sinai."

"Are you sure?"

"Yeah...yeah..."

Kerstin drove me to Mount Sinai Hospital. Night was falling on now-abandoned College Street. On the way, I gazed at the colourful lights of coffee houses and restaurants, and I felt like I didn't belong to the world of people out taking a stroll or having dinner. I'm awfully sick, I said to myself as I peered at my wife's stern profile, so similar to the utterly grim faces I encountered everywhere that day. After a while I commented to myself, That's why they have hospitals. For people like me.

Once on the psychiatric inpatient ward at Mount Sinai, I recognized Linda, the nurse on call, though I hadn't seen her in twenty years. Faintly mumbling, I asked whether she remembered me. After looking me up and down she said, "You've gained weight and lost a lot of hair." She laughed good-naturedly.

Linda showed me my room, the nurses' station, the television, the group therapy room, and the dining area—all the necessary amenities of a psychiatric ward. I followed her in silence. Inexplicably, I said to myself that I wasn't very ill and soon would be discharged from that heinous warehouse of sick souls.

A short while later, Linda, now perched on a swivelling chair, asked me to take a seat. There stood between us a small desk covered with manila envelopes and forms. She held a pen and a clipboard. "I have to do a nursing assessment," she explained.

Another assessment? My recurring battles against my illness had taught me that I'd soon be assessed by a psychiatry resident, a social worker, and an occupational therapist. Would a psychologist now assess me too? At that point I was too sluggish and numb to object to any assessment. But were assessments necessary to establish that I was dead inside?

"What's your last name, Shalom?" Linda had her eyes on a form.

I spelled it out slowly, and she jotted it down.

"Date of birth?"

I took a deep breath before saying, "Today."

She raised her head and peered at me with much concern. "Today?" she asked. "What do you mean?"

I wished I could have smiled. "It's my birthday...today... born nineteen...thirty-nine..."

She smiled soothingly. "Happy birthday! I suppose your family knows about it."

"Oh, yes! We had...lentil salad...for lunch...my favourite. But...right after...I became...very ill.

"I see." Her eyes now scrutinized a form attached to a clipboard. "And your address?"

I told her.

She completed other forms and then discussed my medications. Already at the Clarke's emergency I had begun worrying about somehow not taking my meds at bedtime and spending long hours awake in my bed. When I mumbled those fears, Linda replied that the hospital's pharmacy had all of my pills plus thousands of others. Her cheery and upbeat tone of voice now annoyed me somehow.

I slept deeply that night, but I woke up next morning in a panic, yet content to be in a closed ward. Linda had explained to me that, even if my wife accompanied me, I needed permission to leave the ward. My suicidal thoughts, however, played inside my head like uninterrupted elevator music.

I had breakfast, and soon after took my pills. I shuffled about the ward, and it didn't take long before I felt hollowed out, as if I'd never had any feelings and wouldn't re-experience anything, good or bad.

Back in my room I tried to read the morning paper, but even the headlines wouldn't register. Once more I toured the ward back and forth, then sat in a chair facing the nurses' station. Like an anthropologist immersed in field research, I watched the women and men going up to the station's receptionist, who would then buzz open the door to the ward. I felt worthless and incapable of doing anything that would alleviate the wretchedness festering inside me.

Just as I had anticipated, over the next few days various mental health professionals assessed me. I learned that there would be group therapy twice a week, and occupational therapy three times a week. I wished I were involved in activities all day long, instead of the unending free time that made me succumb to the emptiness taking over my life. I felt doomed to live the rest of my life hollowed out, and blamed myself for it.

Things improved in the evening as Kerstin and Martin visited me. It took me a great deal of effort to engage in coherent conversations. My wife looked tired and worried, and to reassure her I stated that the antidepressant I was on would kick in "in a few days." I was lying, since I knew for certain that no antidepressant ever takes effect in less than three weeks. But I felt it was my duty to put on a brave face, so I lied again when I declared that in a week or so I would be discharged. In my heart I knew I was very ill and likely to remain on the ward for weeks, perhaps even months. My wife and son listened attentively, uttered words of encouragement, but looked like they didn't believe the words coming out of my mouth.

In the following days, friends came to visit me in the evening. Most of them were clinicians that probably understood that my hospitalization meant that I was dangerously suicidal. We chatted about life on the ward, their work and mine, plans for vacations, books they were reading, even the news on TV. It surprised me that my friends referred to my life *after* the hospital stay, since I expected to be locked up to the day I died. The weekend came, and I was allowed to go home from Friday afternoon until Sunday evening.

Despite Kerstin's efforts to make the weekend at home pleasant, my visit turned into a calamity. During Shabbat dinner on Friday, intrusive thoughts of killing her first and then myself began to haunt me. I had no precise plans for the murder-suicide, but it was a fixed idea I couldn't banish. By Saturday at lunch, I could no longer keep my sick thoughts in check, so I shared them with her, and she looked less scared than I'd expected. She reacted calmly, but there was both alarm and dread in her face and her voice. "I'm glad you told me," she said. A while later, she shattered the devastating silence. "Do you want to go back to the ward? I'll be glad to drive you there."

My palms splayed on the table, I leaned forward. "Don't worry," I whispered. "I don't think I'll kill you! I'm too weak to kill a fly. How could I possibly harm you?" I felt grateful that she hadn't panicked.

She looked me deep in the eye, as if seeing me for the first time. "Why don't you call your nurse? They said you could call the ward 24-7."

Over the phone, I told the nurse on call about the murder-suicide idea. It disappointed me that her reaction was to invite me to come to the ward and talk to her. There was neither worry nor alarm in her voice, just a calm, studied reaction to what I'd just shared. I realized I was sicker than I'd thought and the nurse was dealing, effectively, with a thoroughly sick man.

After admitting to my plans, I had nothing else to say, so the nurse broke the silence. "Do you have plans to socialize?"

"No. I saw many friends during the week."

"Get out of the house. Go to a movie, a bar, or a theatre. Show your wife you are in control."

"I feel better now. I love my wife. I'd never harm her."

"Come back to the ward if you feel you can't handle your feelings."

Despite my coherent speech, I knew I was utterly unhinged. I had relied on the nurse on call as if she were an expert on the management of murder-suicide. At the time, whoever listened to me felt like a saviour with all the answers for my condition. On Monday morning, back on the ward, I told the resident and several nurses about my murder-suicide ideations. The resident asked me a few questions about my moods, sleep, and appetite, as if to indicate he wasn't terribly alarmed. The nurse I'd been assigned to peered at me calmly—only mildly interested in what I was saying—then she went on to discuss my plans for the day. I realized I'd overreacted terribly, as the staff wasn't particularly worried about my wife or me. Looking back, I realize I was so weak, so incapacitated, that I was deemed utterly incapable of carrying out a murder-suicide.

The next weekend I again went home on a pass. This time I had no thoughts of killing my wife, though impulses to commit suicide worsened considerably. This pattern continued for six weeks, and my condition barely improved. I believed I would never feel better, and the more time I spent on the ward, the weaker I'd feel.

The truly memorable event in all those weeks was a comment by a social worker. "Jumping in front of a subway train," he told me, "has maimed some people badly, but didn't necessarily kill them." I was flabbergasted to hear that my preferred method of suicide wasn't at all guaranteed to succeed! For years I'd taken for granted that a speeding train would instantaneously put an end to all my suffering. Other methods of committing suicide were also flawed and fraught with the risk of failure, great pain, and lasting physical damage.

Though I remained suicidal after six weeks on the ward, it was decided to discharge me. The idea was for me to resume work gradually, working two hours a day to begin with, and spending nights at the hospital. In hindsight, my therapists had taken a huge risk, as I was still dangerous to myself and yet was expected to ride the subway on my own. Spending hours away from the ward was a prospect I both dreaded and found appealing, and I vowed to follow through with the staff's recommendations.

Once I resumed work at the office, I felt so shaky and vulnerable that I decided to see only the least challenging patients. As I'd done for decades, I informed them I was back at work, but said nothing about my condition or the treatments I was undergoing. The following week, feeling more secure, I saw a few more patients. Suicidal thoughts had receded considerably, and I looked forward to sleeping at home and working full-time. Though I had no doubts I had been discharged to save on the high costs of hospitalization, I also agreed that my discharge had proved effective. Had I stayed longer, it'd have been even harder to wean myself away from my dependency on ward activities and chats with staff.

It astonished me that I hadn't lost a single patient during my absence from work. Some of my colleagues were surprised that no patients of mine had looked for another therapist while I was ill. I explained that almost all my patients had known me for months or years, and hoped to resume therapy as soon as I recovered. Also, I had kept in touch with them over the phone and had given them names of colleagues in case they needed immediate help. My coming back to an intact practice helped me to recover financially and personally, especially since my patients were eager to resume treatment. "I can't be all that bad," I comforted myself.

During my stay at Mount Sinai Hospital, some patients sent me get-well cards, or left phone messages wishing me a speedy recovery. Their good intentions strengthened my belief that my practice was not as endangered as I'd feared. Yes, severe depressions badly affected my thoughts and feelings, but they didn't—as I had anticipated—destroy my career or me. I had had, over the years, a great deal of personal therapy myself and learned what people actually wanted, or needed, to get out of therapy.

ONCE OUT OF THE HOSPITAL, IT WAS VERY HARD FOR ME to write fiction. My concentration was spotty, and I couldn't read even short stories, owing to my wandering mind. In order not to lose touch with inspiring language, I resumed writing down uncommon words and phrases I encountered, and nightly went over the new entries in my notebook.

Once I resumed therapy with Dr. Graham, she wouldn't tolerate any claims that I was too sick to write well.

"Write!" she insisted. "You'll feel better about yourself. It'll improve your mood."

"I can't," I implored. "I'm not well enough. No ideas for stories ever enter my head."

"Do it gradually," she replied, sweetly but firmly. "Every day, write a few minutes. With time, you'll find the wherewithal to turn out a whole story."

"I can't!" I yelled, her insistence raising my hackles. "Too much, you're demanding too much!"

At the end of that session she handed me a page with *Homework* as its heading. She had written down that I must sit at the computer twenty minutes every morning and write at least one paragraph. Upon encountering the blank computer monitor, I decided that, since I had no choice but to write, I might as well work on a story about winning a lottery. At the time, I was weekly buying lottery tickets, and intensely daydreamed of what I would do with the millions coming my way.

I decided to make good use of my gloom and pessimism by writing a cautionary tale of a man winning thirty-five million dollars in a lottery, only to realize that from the day he collected his millions his life had become a nightmare. Dreaming up distresses and misfortunes for the suddenly rich man occurred to me easily; almost joyfully, I came up with misery after misery. I mailed the final draft of the story to Susan Ioannou, my editor, and informed her that I'd written the story for therapy purposes and it lacked literary merit. The edited manuscript came back with Susan's recommendation to submit it for publication, since she did find the story meritorious enough. My editor felt I'd captured the irony of a winning ticket that drives its holder into paranoia and leads to loss of friendships, career, and peace of mind. Eventually, it appeared in a small literary magazine, and I included it in a collection of stories published in 2006. Henceforth, I felt capable of writing publishable material even while moderately depressed.

Dr. Graham built upon that success and urged me to write a story about an overweight man and his failure to lose weight. At the time, I was overeating, and writing about that problem might be very helpful, Dr. Graham declared. I couldn't, unfortunately, come up with a reasonable plot or a convincing character for a story, and it took me a whole year to lose ten pounds.

Despite the return to work and gradual recovery, my sense of utter helplessness remained. Again, I experienced difficulty with paperwork at home and at the office, and I lagged behind in reviewing financial matters. As the idea of doing work around the house still petrified me, Kerstin shouldered the burden of cooking, cleaning, and making sure our apartment was in working order. Months after my stay at Mount Sinai Hospital, I wrote a story of a man so profoundly helpless that he couldn't help his wife with chores around the house. His demanding wife and insistent therapist advocated positive thinking and an active lifestyle—exactly what the sick man couldn't manage. Eventually, the protagonist musters courage enough to attend a class reunion, where he meets a high school sweetheart, but is at a loss for words and cannot open up to her. The narrative ends with the main character failing to communicate with his wife and his therapist, both of them uncompromising figures. Titled "A Dry Depression" after the narrator's inability to shed tears, the story appeared in *The Dalhousie Review*, a fine magazine that had previously published two of my stories.

This and other successes convinced me that writing fiction is about creating works of art, with any therapeutic effect being serendipitous, illusory, or transient. Writing to obtain relief from mental disorders is a weak, largely ineffective therapy. Instead, a regime of antidepressants and psychotherapy has many times more to offer, in my view. Oftentimes, a lot of the kvetching about traumas, abuses, and addictions is a piteous attempt to avoid emotionally painful, but quite effective, treatments. In this regard, I feel sorry for well-meaning, empathetic readers who are exploited by sensationalists that foist their repugnant self-pity on unsuspecting audiences.

The kitchen sink was the battlefield where my daily wars against passivity and helplessness took place. And no less harmful were the self-deprecations and abuse I lavished on myself. Dinner over, I would panic as I faced the pile of dishes, greasy pots, and dirty pans marinating in the sink. Entirely disgusted and paralyzed, I felt unable to move a finger, though Kerstin had prepared the entire dinner. My sense of fairness compelled me to contribute, such as washing all pots and dishes. But, instead, I struggled with voices inside my head violently protesting, "I can't do it! I can't! I can't!" as stomach knots badly hurt me. My compassionate and understanding wife would gently shunt me aside, don latex gloves, and do all the chores I could not. Yet her magnanimity made me feel even more incompetent, and more defeated.

Often I felt so embarrassed over my condition that I ruthlessly forced myself to scrub a pot clean. One way of saying "force myself" in Hebrew is *oness at atzmi*. The verb *oness* means not only force but, in some contexts, rape too. Indeed, I felt I was raping myself when, against my will, I was doing repulsive chores. The battle would last about forty minutes, till the sink and all its contents had been cleaned. My flimsy feelings of pride didn't last long, and the next day the paralyzing inner voices would assail me again.

Dr. Graham would exclaim "Whoopee!" every time I reported on a success of sorts. Time and again, she provided encouragement, such as "Keep trying! Do it again! If you don't take care of chores, life will become even harder!" Although her exhortations filled me with good intentions, the mere sight of a congested sink filled me with dread. Only by the spring of 2007 did I manage to clean the dishes about two-thirds of the time—an improvement, I conceded.

Only my wife, sons, and a few close friends knew of my struggling with an utter sense of disempowerment laced with sickly passivity. Outside the home, I wore the mask of a competent therapist who wrote fiction in his spare time. I may have fooled some friends, who believed I was very ill but still "functioning" somehow. In those bleak years, the word "uxorious" accurately described me and the life I was living.

The pitiable clinging to my wife drastically worsened one evening while I was still spending nights at the hospital. One afternoon, after I'd seen three patients in therapy, Kerstin was supposed to pick me up at 5:30 by my office. I waited by the curb, but she didn't show up. Time passed, and acute anxiety made me hyperventilate. "Has something happened?" I asked myself, gasping, "Was she hurt on the way here? Is she in a hospital?" An overwhelming dread came over me.

By six o'clock, after I'd called home several times and got no answer, I persuaded myself that she'd died in a car accident. I began feeling abandoned, paralyzed, and cosmically lonely. Shuddering by the curb, I watched cars passing by, the belief that she'd been killed growing stronger and stronger. I mentally composed a lengthy, elaborate script about her death, her funeral, my grief, and what I'd say in my eulogy. So engrossed was I with my anguish that I did not feel sorry for her; I could only think of how miserable my life would become once my crutch had abruptly been removed. I felt so sorry for myself that I wished I could weep like a toddler whose mother had mysteriously vanished.

The denouement of my overdramatic scenario was anticlimactic: Kerstin passed by my office at 6:30 and picked up what was by then a frozen statue of her husband. There had been a misunderstanding: she thought we'd agreed to meet at 6:30, an hour later than what I'd told myself. Once seated in the passenger's scat beside her, I was still so convinced I'd become a widower that I couldn't celebrate my wife's presumed rebirth.

Whenever panic attacks born of dread strike me, I compose fantastic scenarios of devastating losses, defeat, and scalding shame. As a psychologist, I've helped scores of people to recognize how they "write," "rewrite," and "edit" petrifying scripts of never-ending suffering. After they calm down a bit, I teach them techniques for fighting back their propensity to capitulate to the figments of their own imagination. What I've never shared with my patients is that my ability to quickly detect their disabling scenarios and train them to fight back is based on my own quite similar struggles.

Months after my discharge from Mount Sinai Hospital, after seeing my last patient on a Friday afternoon, I decided to "work" on my phone. I had in mind woolly and indistinct notions of controlling the entire telephone system, not necessarily to speak with anyone in particular. To put my ideas to a test, I called home but got no answer. Then I attempted to contact people in Toronto and abroad, but failed, inexplicably. In a frenzy, I punched and punched my phone's little keyboard, but the more buttons I pushed, the less competent I felt and the more erratic I became.

In the meantime, my wife called me, as I was very late for Shabbat dinner. After repeatedly calling my office, she realized my phone was dead, and she feared I was in the throes of a mood swing. She got in touch with Peter Herschman, who rushed to my office only to meet with an entirely manic person who couldn't explain why he was so frenziedly experimenting with the phone. He drove me to the emergency of the Clarke Institute, where I raised hell by shouting nonstop: "I'm a Jewish doctor! I'm a Jewish doctor!"

I was entirely ignored, then referred to the emergency of Toronto East General Hospital, where my continual yelling didn't at all impress the hospital's staff. Their attitude disappointed me, as I craved admiration and recognition. My loud, crazed self-presentation failed to rouse any interest in people waiting to see a doctor either, and once again I was completely ignored. The more unacknowledged I felt, the louder I hollered, since it infuriated me to be so totally disregarded.

That manic episode ended prosaically, once a male attendant escorted me to the psychiatric ward while I continued to boast and brag. Once placed in an isolation room, a male nurse asked me to slide down my pants so he could give me an injection of Haldol, an antipsychotic. Within minutes, the drug made me feel so sleepy that I stretched out on that cell's narrow iron bed and soon fell asleep. I slept until eight o'clock the next morning, and the coffee I had for breakfast was cold and bitter. I realized I'd been grandiloquently psychotic, and my insane hollering embarrassed me a great deal.

Hours later, a psychiatrist I was well acquainted with examined me, and we agreed that my manic wave had completely died down. I asked to be discharged, but he said he'd rather wait until the next morning. On Sunday, I was allowed to leave the hospital, after about thirty-six hours on the ward, my shortest hospitalization ever, a feat made possible by advances in psychopharmacology.

Though still shaken by the manic wave, the next morning I went to work. At the time, I had a psychologist in group therapy who was on staff at Toronto East General. It worried me that she might find out about my disturbance and hospitalization, but during the group session she displayed no signs of being upset. I had no idea whether or not she knew about my breakdown, or whether she had chosen not to discuss my illness for fear of violating my privacy.

In the following two years, I was in and out of hospitals several times, but my work continued rather smoothly, and I attended shul services Saturday mornings. The services proved a beneficial distraction from the onsets of depression that hollowed me out. But my lifetime secular stance persisted, and it bothered my wife. Our congregation, incidentally, allowed our rabbi to perform same-sex marriages, the first in Toronto to do so. I felt comfortable with my charitable, progressively minded congregants, and, despite my difficulty in making small talk, I managed to socialize with a number of the shul-goers.

The Saturday services were very repetitive, and I frequently nodded off during the reading of the Torah and again during the sermon. My dozing, I assumed, must have been common knowledge, since I was unable to conceal it. Since the members of my congregation knew me mostly while I was unwell, they became acquainted with a man who smiled infrequently, rarely laughed, and almost never initiated conversations. My frozen face and ungainly conduct probably led some to believe I was a hopeless case of underdeveloped social skills. They must have wondered how I could make a living as a psychotherapist, given my laconicism and bamboo-like stiffness. And it was no help that the shul's social hall was a low-ceilinged basement with poor acoustics, and my hearing loss led me to schmooze only with people that stood up physically close to me. In all, my fellow shul members must have thought me a rather piteous figure, while they liked my personable and communicative wife a lot.

About 2001, when I was sixty-two, I observed a marked change in my practice. People applying for services were reluctant to engage in long-term, elaborate treatments. They looked for speedy solutions to their problems—what some colleagues contemptuously referred to as "quick fixes." It became difficult to find people interested in learning the significance of their dreams and fantasies over weeks and months; gone were the glories of therapists delighting in theory-based, clever interpretations. Typically, people wanted a pragmatic, problem-solving treatment that would last—and cost—as little as possible. The demand for cognitive behaviour therapy soared, as the public somehow believed that successful treatment of "negative thoughts" necessitated two dozen sessions, on average.

The change in patients' world views was noticeable: they entered therapy to obtain relief from painful situations, such as the breakup of a relationship. There was little demand for profound, potentially life-altering insights, or interest in exploring the meaning of their lives. Despite wishes to engage in brief therapies, many patients presented lifelong issues, or suffered from harrowing mental illnesses. For those people, once-a-week therapy sessions, though expensive, were a necessary shot in the arm that kept them working and experiencing a reasonably enjoyable life after hours.

As time passed, I became less and less engaged in my professional career and spent long hours writing. I stopped giving workshops in group therapy, a productive way of making myself known to potential referral sources. And then, following my recurring mood swings, Dr. Parikh and Dr. Graham, independently from one another, recommended that I work no more than twenty hours a week. Though I had always risen to the occasion and did acceptable work, even while disordered, I began to feel tired and emotionally drained after a day's work. I no longer looked forward to treating "difficult" patients, and began experiencing them as demanding and wearisome people. And yet

I dreaded the day I would close my office for good, as I'd had a private office for more than four decades and experienced it as my turf, writer's lair, and impregnable bunker. Nearly all of my fiction was written in my office—what led me to say to myself, "The day I have no office of my own, and no patients to assess and treat, will be a dispiriting landmark." Aging friends of mine admitted to experiencing, on and off, the same melancholy.

Chapter 10

Drinking, Drugs, Death, and Dirges

Over time, Daniel's excessive drinking worsened. Even while visiting us at our condo, he'd drink tall glass and after tall glass of vodka mixed with cranberry juice. We knew he was an alcoholic and many times offered to pay for his therapy, but he declined, insisting there was nothing wrong with him. He scoffed at the idea of treatment, claiming that I, for example, offered nothing but costly bullshit to my patients. He spent much time and money in bars, and the jokes he told me reminded me of drunks I'd seen in movies and on television. I felt out-and-out impotent, as I saw him as a sick man in need of professional help. But as he would have no treatment, my hands were tied. And yet, despite the heavy drinking, Daniel managed to keep a rather responsible position with a decent salary. I dreaded the day he'd lose his job on account of his heavy drinking.

As Daniel's condition deteriorated, Kerstin and I argued more. She blamed herself for Daniel's intemperance, even though I maintained she'd been a loving and devoted mother—many times more than my hard-to-reach, often less than lukewarm mother. But in my wife's mind, her working full-time, instead of being a stay-at-home mother, was the cause of Daniel's problems. Arguing with her led us nowhere, as she would accuse herself of having neglected our sons. Though genuine, at times she sounded as if she were parodying psychoanalytic theories, such as insisting that the only reason for Daniel's problems was his mother's flawed mothering. Innumerable times I argued that, since her guilt was pathological, she was in dire need of therapy. She maintained, however, that her guilt was heartfelt and genuine, and no treatment would ever change the way she felt. I dreaded our recurring arguments, since the fragile balance between sanity and lunacy I lived with might unravel, and a severe depression would assail me. Kerstin's perennial guilt weighed on me, and only my bursts of anger would silence her.

In the fall of 2005, Daniel was fired from his job. He readily admitted that his work performance had been poor and his dismissal justified. Before searching for a new position, he went on vacation to the Dominican Republic and upon return admitted to having experienced panic attacks and asked to stay in our apartment, which we agreed to unconditionally. He sounded a bit paranoid, claiming that his condo's electrical wiring was faulty and that his feet were scalding hot at times. He then confessed to using cocaine, in addition to drinking. While with us, he slept for several days, as if to make up for sleep deprivation. He admitted to feeling quite disturbed while on vacation.

Kerstin and I arranged for Daniel to start residential treatment at the Bellwood Treatment Centre. He was, however, kicked out after two weeks because of an entry in his diary advocating the hiring of thugs that would beat up the centre's director. He refused to have further treatment and, instead, began attending AA meetings. For a while he seemed to be abstaining from drinking.

One Friday evening, Kerstin and I had another heated argument about our son, with no new ideas expressed. She again elaborated on Daniel's hardships and on her blame and guilt. I suddenly began shouting and withdrew to our bedroom for fear of assaulting her. As wave after wave of rage kept washing over me, I was unable to calm down. Instead of taking my bedtime medication and falling asleep in less than half an hour, I lay in bed, possessed by fantasies of strangling my wife and avenging something so vague that I couldn't define it. In a rage, I jumped out of bed and strode to the living room. Kerstin was on the balcony, smoking, while Martin, our firstborn, was in our study on the computer. Wordlessly, I slid the door to the balcony open, entered it, and with a clenched fist pounded my wife's head. She bent forward, moaning, "You're killing me. You're killing me." I howled back accusations I can't recall, and suddenly I noticed Martin beside me on the balcony. Unwilling, as usual, to become involved in his parents' arguments, he cool-headedly ordered me, "Leave Mum alone! Right now!"

For long hours I lay in bed that night, unable to keep my rage in check. Endlessly, I fantasized strangling my wife, or beating her up until she bled like a broken faucet. It didn't even occur to me that I loved her dearly when I was well; only my fantasies of revenge mattered. Soon I began dreaming up scenarios of being locked up in an institution for the criminally insane for murdering my wife of forty years. It pleased me, perversely, to think that, on account of my disorder, I wouldn't be charged with first-degree murder but would instead be locked up in a psychiatric hospital. I pictured expressionless attendants ramming fifteen pills down my throat every day. And, instead of kind and empathetic therapists, a robotic, cold-hearted psychiatrist would monthly reassess me. My registration as a psychologist, I imagined, would be revoked for good.

I slept fitfully that night after a massive dose of tranquilizers. Still groggy in the morning, I found Kerstin asleep in the living room on our couch. Instantaneously, I realized I'd been through a gruesome mood swing, for which I felt immensely guilty. I offered heartfelt apologies, which did not allay her fear of being battered again.*

Over the next few days, I started doubting whether I was genuinely ill when I assaulted my wife. Indeed, I'd experienced a potent disturbance when I attacked my wife, but was I psychotic or merely enraged? I began to agonize over issues of responsibility and accountability for my conduct. After all, I told myself, not every outburst of rage is due to mental illness. Even indisputably sane people may lose control over themselves and lash out at loved ones. Did I assault my wife because I was certifiably mad, or was it a huge temper tantrum over my incapacity to control her? After a slew of sleepless nights, I decided to take full responsibility for the assault and seek help.

Days later, my wife and I met with Dr. Parikh, who referred us to a marital therapist. That was the second time in my mental-illness career that *three* therapists were treating me: Dr. Parikh monitoring my medications and overall well-being; Dr. Graham providing psychotherapy with a cognitive bent; and the new therapist,

---

* My wife, incidentally, was very loyal to me and supported me emotionally, even when I abused her verbally or threatened to kill her. Only once did she say she needed a break from me, mentioning renting an apartment for herself, where she could reflect on whether or not to continue living with me. Our sons wouldn't hear of it, and told her I was seriously ill and needed her badly. She rented no apartment and continued living with me, and I was very grateful to our sons.

Ms. Carol Parker, a social worker, mediating between me and my wife.

A week later we saw Carol Parker at her office. She was about fifty and wore no makeup except for pencilling her eyebrows. Her eyes expressed softness and kindness. She was a sharp dresser, and I never saw her wearing the same outfit twice. The silver jewellery she favoured indicated that she, like my wife, loved Georg Jensen designs.

Carol was soft-spoken and said little. She de-emphasized my physical assault, gently steering the conversation into an exploration of miscommunications between us. In the sessions, Kerstin wept intensely as she spoke of her unrelenting guilt about Daniel's drinking and seldom mentioned other concerns. I initiated most discussions, since my wife seemed tongue-tied and didn't quite know what material to bring up. After decades of therapy, and my work experience as a psychologist, I readily conversed with healers of all denominations.

Six months later, I felt we'd reached a plateau and decided to end the treatment, since Kerstin and I had arrived at a better understanding of one another. We agreed that my wife would continue seeing Carol in individual therapy, as they'd developed a good rapport. In the past, Kerstin had given two male psychiatrists a try but had never felt they were of any help to her.

While marital therapy was going on, my relationship with Daniel had markedly improved. I stopped berating him and his drinking and rarely showed anger toward him.

He was, as a rule, tolerant of my mood swings, and at times had mimicked and poked fun at my self-absorbed, lengthy silences. He began kidding with me, and told me jokes he'd heard in bars. Encouraged by those moves, I frequently hugged and kissed him. He wouldn't reject me, as I had feared, and faintly reciprocated my displays of affection.

One evening, I mustered courage and turned to him. "Daniel," I said, "you and I are getting along better. So the time has come for us to discuss how I abused you and gave you a hard time while I was ill."

His nostrils flared, and his brow furrowed. "What abuse, Dad? You never abused Martin or me."

Flabbergasted, I pleaded, "But Daniel, I took a knife to your throat! Many times I heaped emotional abuse on you when I was sick. Don't you remember?"

"Dad," he vigorously waved, as if to get rid of a pestering mosquito, "you never hit me. There was no abuse!"

My feelings of guilt promptly dismissed, I whispered, "That's right, I didn't beat up on you or your brother. But what about my outbursts, my screaming? Once, when I barked loudly, you said I belonged in a hospital—and you were right!"

"Yes, we had our differences," he forcefully contended, "but I was a smart-ass and a difficult teenager. Yes, I gave you a hard time. But I'm telling you, Dad, you *never* beat me up! So why are you talking about abuse?"

I gave up. Daniel almost desperately cleaved to the notion that he grew up in a "normal" home, that his father never abused him, that his father's outbursts took place because of the son's rebelliousness. He'd rather blame himself than acknowledge that he may have sustained emotional abuse. Like a six-year-old, he held onto the belief that his was a healthy family; that his parents loved him and had done no wrong. I felt at once deflated and puzzled by his thinking. In my heart, I was unambiguously certain I had abused him verbally while I was ill, and once was close to slitting his throat. My son's distortions and denials made me feel even guiltier, as he gave me no opportunity to express my festering shame, guilt, and self-blame.

On November 15, 2006, I spent the entire morning assessing a patient, and only by lunchtime did I notice that there was a message on my phone. Upon retrieving it, I heard Kerstin, immensely distraught, asking me to come home right away. "Something terrible happened," she said. "Daniel is dead."

Short of breath and heart pounding, I called her. She cried bitterly and again urged me to come home right away, because, she reaffirmed, Daniel had died. I stormed out of the office without locking the door or turning the lights off, feeling dazed and disoriented. I ran home, wending my way through groups of office workers on their lunch break. What happened? I asked myself, in terror. Why would my wife say that our son was dead? How can I help her? Or him?

Once at home, it surprised me that Martin was not at work but in our condo. Crying continually, Kerstin informed me that, since she hadn't heard from Daniel for three days, she went to his building, introduced herself to the concierge, and asked her to open the door to his apartment. The young woman escorted her to the sixteenth floor and unlocked Daniel's door. Kerstin rushed to his bedroom, calling out his name, but didn't find him there. Then she heard the concierge exclaiming from the living room, "He's here!"

Kerstin strode toward the concierge and saw Daniel sprawled on the carpeted floor, blood on his face and on the maroon rug we had stitched when he was a child. She knelt down, hugging and kissing him. His face, however, was blue and his body cold.

"Call an ambulance!" she shrieked.

"I'm afraid it's too late," the concierge said.

My wife called Martin and told him about the death of his brother. In minutes he came to Daniel's apartment. He wept but didn't want to look at his dead brother's body. Soon the police and two medics arrived. They asked if Daniel was a drug addict, and Martin confirmed that his brother used cocaine. Pictures were taken, our dead son was loaded onto a stretcher and hauled away. The next day, a policeman advised us that an autopsy would be performed, as Daniel had died at home, not in a hospital.

I wept as I listened to Kerstin, something I hadn't done for ages, my melancholies invariably dry and tearless. And since that heartrending day, I haven't shed a single tear, my mourning and sadness always arid.

That day we had a skimpy lunch, and the entire afternoon and evening we sat in the living room, going over photos of Daniel and saying very little. We felt incapable of making arrangements for a funeral. We didn't—couldn't—contact friends, and silently agreed to restrict the grief and suffering to the three of us.

Only the next morning did it occur to Kerstin to contact Rabbi Elkin, the spiritual leader of the Narayever congregation. He and his wife Linda joined us in a few minutes. The rabbi took upon himself all necessary arrangements for Daniel to be buried at our shul's cemetery, though he'd never been a member of the congregation. Kerstin and I contacted a funeral home regarding burial and funerary services.

That evening, Peter Herschman and his wife Pat kept us company and comforted us. They were a great source of emotional support the following week. Meanwhile, the coroner's office let us know over the phone that Daniel's cause of death was unclear. The final results of the autopsy, we were told, would not be known for months. We felt numb and out of touch with the tragedy, and considered various theories about what had caused Daniel's death, but came up with nothing specific or convincing.

Next day I wrote a eulogy for Daniel, the most difficult, most painful writing I have ever done. I decided to mention that in the last years of his life he had battled the demons of addiction to cocaine and painkillers.

As expected, the funeral and shivah were profoundly sad events. Kerstin and I were confused, still in shock, and mechanically responded to those around us. People came to our home to comfort us, and prayers took place in the evening. Those ceremonies numbed our pain, and true bereavement would come over us only weeks later. Meanwhile, I was in disbelief, and while on the street I would spot someone looking "just like Daniel," as if he'd miraculously returned to life. I even "heard" his voice from time to time. Even before I was back at work, I concluded, with a lot of self-hatred, that I hadn't supported Daniel enough, such as telling him that my outbursts didn't put an end to my love for him. It was devastating to realize there would be no opportunities to correct my mistakes. He was gone, forever.

The finality of Daniel's death came as an unsettling, violent insight. I'd never see him again, hear him exclaim "city morgue!" whenever he picked up the phone in his apartment. Never again would I laugh at his rambunctious jokes. I compiled a long list of things that would never reoccur.

Despite my guilt and grief, I didn't blame myself. Decades of therapy had enabled me to mourn deeply but without pointing fingers or flagellating myself. I immersed myself in the irreparable loss I'd incurred, rather than blame myself for my son's death. Every picture of my dead son made me feel as if a frozen forefinger and thumb were tweaking my heart. I mourned but didn't experience the waves of grief that drove my wife to shed bitter tears. She is, as a rule, guilt-prone, and now that our son had died she blamed herself. Over and over she held that it was her fault he'd become an alcoholic and an addict. All attempts to reason with her were in vain. She saw Carol Parker in therapy every week but doubted whether it was helping. I insisted that she continue her treatment indefinitely, since we could easily afford it.

Martin took care of his brother's estate and the arrangements concerning Daniel's employer and bank. While working on Daniel's bank account, our older son found out that, two weeks prior to his death, Daniel had cashed thousands of dollars. It was clear that our son had not been free of alcohol and drugs after all, and relapsed badly right before he died. Why else would he need all that money?

All our hopes and dreams of Daniel having freed himself of substance abuse collapsed like a house of cards once he died. Our son was an addict and had died of an overdose of a variety of street drugs. I insisted that he didn't commit suicide, as he was in a relatively good mood in the months preceding his death. To buttress my views, I invoked my expertise, not as a psychologist but as a person who had for many years waged wars on impulses to kill himself.

We got the pathologist's report months after Daniel's death. The diagnosis was unambiguous and came as no surprise: mixed drug intoxication. And yet to read it stated in writing was devastating. We shuddered at the pathologist's reporting the precise weight of Daniel's heart and brain, as if our son had been hacked to pieces. The report confirmed that our son had been a sick man who died of too much cocaine and painkillers. We experienced no comfort when we learned that there were no traces of alcohol in his blood. Apparently, Daniel had resisted vodka the last few months of his life, one reason why we believed he had temporarily overcome his affliction. And his brother didn't know of his drug addiction either, so skilful was Daniel's concealment.

The death of a child is so brutal, so final. It exterminates all hopes that you'll ever see your son grow and develop, marry, have children, and enjoy a gratifying career. The passing of a parent, in my experience, is a relatively minor event compared to the death of a child. The latter feels absurd, arbitrary, cruel, and unnatural. It does make sense, somehow, when a parent dies before his or her offspring, even though that death may rob you of a large portion of your past. The death of a child demolishes your future. Eventually, the deceased child becomes a memory, but no longer a source of hope and loving anticipations.

It surprised me, at the time, how well people understood the agony of losing a child. One of Daniel's friends, a young man whose wife was expecting their first child, came to visit us during the shivah, and commented that the death of a child is what all parents dread the most. He admitted to having fears of losing his yet-unborn child.

Many friends supported us by stating that the death of a child is the worst thing that could ever happen to them. And yet it was remarkable to notice how aware people seemed to be about the devastation Kerstin and I were going through. Peter Herschman said we'd never forget our son, and his death would be with us forever. His observation was an expression of heartfelt compassion, no doubt. One of Kerstin's fears, and a reason for her excessive guilt, was the dread she might forget our son unless she thought of him day and night. Stating and restating the permanence of our loss was her way of fighting back worries about Daniel's death becoming an obscure blur.

I resumed work ten days after Daniel's death, and some months later resumed writing fiction and other routines. My heart, however, felt like it was shrinking painfully whenever I heard news of my friends' children. Even ten years later, I still experience strong emotions whenever I catch sight of pictures I took of Daniel, especially one of him as a teenager joyously smiling at the camera. I keep portraits of him at home and the office, and I'm convinced that only death will put an end to the melancholy that comes over me whenever I recall my son dying long before me. I'm no masochist. And yet I don't want the pain and longing for my son to go away. As I continue to mourn him, I feel real, substantial, and whole.

Chapter 11

Um Santo Remédio

THE ABOVE CHAPTER TITLE IS A COMMON EXPRESSION in Portuguese, my first language. At times I feel tempted to translate it plainly as "a holy medication," or even "a holy drug." Those translations, however, fail to capture what this phrase has always meant to me.

I first heard it from the maids my mother employed in Rio de Janeiro, in the 1940s and early 1950s, when even middle-class families could afford a full-time, live-in *empregada*. Then, even small apartments featured quarters for those women: a puny bedroom with a narrow bed, a minuscule dresser, and a single chair. They worked long hours, those maids, cleaning the apartment, cooking, doing the laundry, and taking care of young children. They rarely complained, at times even felt lucky, since they descended from poor, illiterate families in the countryside; living in my mother's home meant they never went to bed hungry. They met and dated young men born and bred in Rio, always more worldly than the bumpkins they'd grown up with.

As for medications, some of those maids had their own ideas on how to treat certain ailments. Stomach aches, for example, were treated with tea prepared from a nectar made from orange blossoms. I was never informed where one could buy that nectar; all I ever heard were reports on it taking away stomach pains, a claim corroborated by vigorously massaging one's navel and eyes exuding gratitude. That a miracle of sorts had taken place was said in whispers, eyes gazing at the ceiling in case we were indoors, or staring heavenward when the maids and I stood by the stairs to my parents' home, watching the world go by.

It didn't escape me that my parents and my brother took no such remedies ever, as they consulted the family doctor in case of pains or fevers. A doctor's visit was something a domestic couldn't afford; the treatments they swore by were, on the other hand, inexpensive and prescribed by friends and acquaintances. My brother, then a medical student and an ardent communist, would dismiss with a wave any magical or holy potions. He vehemently denounced them as emblems of the rapacious exploitation of the working class that a Bolshevik-like revolution would put an end to.

In the fall of 2010, when I was seventy-one, Dr. Parikh announced, even before asking how I had been feeling, that the drug Seroquel had been approved by Health Canada as a treatment for bipolar disorder. He seemed quite excited, as he explained how the drug worked: "It's a widely used antidepressant," he declared, "but I recommend you take large doses of it. The drug will act as an antipsychotic; you'll be sleeping better, and you may soon be feeling less depressed."

For thirty years I had tried at least eight antidepressants. A few helped me sleep better, others made me gain weight, and Paxil, as mentioned, lifted my moods but eventually drove me into mania. For decades I had been a compliant patient, doing whatever my doctors recommended; so at bedtime I began ingesting the new drug, even though I wasn't very hopeful. Bouts of depression came over me frequently and seemingly at random, and all efforts to bring them under pharmacological control had failed. My serious depressions continued to impinge on my entire life.

Within days, I learned that Seroquel allowed me to sleep long hours, but I awoke groggy and in a daze, my mouth as dry as sandpaper. It could take thirty minutes before I felt alert enough to face the day. This went on for a few months until one day I realized I had not been depressed since I began taking the new medication, and no foul moods had been spoiling my life after-hours. When I shared all this with Dr. Parikh, he commented, quite excitedly, "It looks like Seroquel is kicking in!"

Today, after eight years of no clinical depressions whatsoever, I can declare that Seroquel is my *santo remédio*, my holy saviour, though I don't massage my navel nor thank

God for the miraculous turn my life has taken. Yes, hypomanic episodes still recur from time to time, but they're relatively mild; I may become overly talkative and argumentative, but without succumbing to violent impulses. Occasionally, I still go on shopping sprees, but these days I "blow" two hundred dollars at most.

Now that disabling moods no longer trouble me, work feels less draining, and I look forward to seeing my patients. My writing has improved, and I have embarked upon an ambitious novel—my swan song, in all likelihood. I was complimented on the pictures of flowers I had taken and enlarged considerably.

Another major change Seroquel brought about was no longer feeling a need to attend Shabbat services at our shul. As stated, not one day in my long life have I believed there is a God somewhere, anywhere. And yet for twelve years I accompanied my wife to Saturday morning services, as they helped me cope with grievous mood swings. But once my black despair lifted, I no longer experienced inner pressure to attend religious services. And I attribute my recovery not to God on high but to the medical researchers that created scientific evidence that Seroquel can be of much help to some bipolar people.

But is the medication I ingest nightly an unfailing solution to the calamitous moods bipolar people must contend with? I seriously doubt it. Different people, with different brain chemistry and genetic loading, may not be as lucky as I have been. Moreover, I cannot declare with certainty that my pathologically low moods are a thing of the past; I surely know they *may* come back. The only valid assertion I can make is that I may have won a battle, but the war is not over, and may never be. I periodically remind myself that bipolar disorder is a beastly, debilitating disease for which there is no cure, only remedies that help.

And yet I am so grateful that my depressions have been tamed that I have thought of writing an ode to the drug that radically changed my life. I envisioned it as a paean to the researchers who painstakingly investigated the drug that wholly transformed my life and made it worthwhile. However, I have yet to pen that poem, since I fear the pharmaceutical company that developed the drug might use it to crassly advertise on TV that nowadays there is a miraculous remedy for bipolar disorder.

Psychotherapy helped me, and cognitive therapy even more so. But those therapies changed my life relatively little compared to the changes Seroquel brought about. Were I a Brazilian maid, I would daily thank God's divine intervention, as the blessed five white pills I ingest at bedtime keep depressions out of my life. They enable me to enjoy life in the company of my family, friends, and patients.

And were researchers to produce evidence that it is beneficial for bipolar people to massage their navels clockwise and piously gaze heavenward, I might initially smile but would soon follow such recommendations faithfully.

Acknowledgements

SUSAN IOANNOU, A CANADIAN POET, HELPFULLY EDITED the first draft of this book. She had previously edited dozens of my stories and patiently taught me how to write fiction in English.

Martin, my son, superbly edited the final version of this memoir. He identified stylistic errors and suggested better, more precise, and more concise alternatives.

Sean Prpick, a trade editor with University of Regina Press, made warm and helpful comments that improved my writing and refined the message I wanted to convey.

About the Author

SHALOM CAMENIETZKI WAS BORN INTO A JEWISH FAMily in Brazil in 1939. As a teenager, he immigrated with his parents to Israel, where he attended high school, did his military service in the Israeli artillery, and then studied for his undergraduate degree at Tel Aviv University. He completed his PhD in psychology in the United States and began his career as a clinical psychologist there, then in Israel, and finally in Toronto, where he has worked most of his adult life. Throughout his career he experienced considerable success in helping mentally ill patients, while also suffering from his own severe bipolar disorder, requiring frequent hospitalizations. Fortunately, for most of the last decade he's been in recovery, thanks to advances in modern drug treatment. He continues to provide individual and group psychotherapy, as well as couples counselling in Toronto (www.shalomcamenietzki.ca).

A Note on the Type

This book is set in Freight Text Pro, designed by Joshua Darden. Clean and highly legible, this font family has its roots firmly planted in a humanist design aesthetic. It was designed with the reader in mind and is ideal for use as a text font in situations of extended viewing, such as in periodicals or data-intensive documents.

The Regina Collection

Named as a tribute to Saskatchewan's capital city with its rich history of boundary-defying innovation, *The Regina Collection* builds upon University of Regina Press's motto of "a voice for many peoples." Intimate in size and beautifully packaged, these books aim to tell the stories of those who have been caught up in social and political circumstances beyond their control.

To see other books in *The Regina Collection*
visit *www.uofrpress.ca*